KEEPING THE SPARK ALIVE

A HELPFUL GUIDE TO IMPROVE ROMANCE IN RELATIONSHIPS

CHLOE CASTILLO

To all those publishers who have rejected my work in the past, who encouraged me to do better.

Contents

CHAPTER ONE

Introduction

Getting married or getting into a relationship is easy. Now there are many people who struggle to get a partner and they may disagree with what I have to say. But this book is not about them. Or maybe it is. But not entirely about them. This book is more about those who have been fortunate enough to find a partner in their lives. And this could be any partner. Whatever orientation you identify with, whatever pronouns you choose to use, whatever your gender, race, color, education status, financial status, age (of course, provided it is above the age of consent) - anything. If you have a partner this book is for you.

This book is more for you if you have a partner and are happy in your relationship but want to find more ways to keep them happy. And this book is more for you if you have a partner and are reaching a state of stability bordering on the mundane or boring with them and want to reignite the spark. However, this book is most for you if you have a partner and are beginning to have disagreements with them that are impacting your relationship adversely. While this book is all about finding new ways to help give that nudge to your relationship, it is important to consider taking professional help such as couples' therapy or relationship counseling if tips and tricks don't seem to cut it anymore. There is no replacement to actual hardcore action-oriented counseling and do not fall into the trap of reading books after books in the hope that things will change miraculously.

That said, this book is aimed at both partners and hence, it would be great if both partners are involved and read the book together to get the most out of it. So, here is what you can expect from the book. The book is loosely divided into two parts. The first part is about all the information you need about the whys and whats of a good relationship. This is as Indians call it, the *'gyaan'* section of the book. This will tell you about what you need to do, what you should not do, why you need to do it, pitfalls to be aware of and myths that you should not fall prey to. This section is a rich section with some nuanced advice and should be read from end-to-end to understand what changes you may perhaps need to make in the relationship.

The second section which has only one chapter (the last one) is about the various practical, tried and tested romantic gestures that you can do for one another to rekindle the passion that you felt for each other when you first got into the relationship. The ideas here include ideas of all types and not just those that burn a hole in your pocket. The objective finally is to make sure that the love blooms again and does not lead you into poverty in the bargain. I hope you find the book useful. I will be happy if you could leave a review for this on Amazon. So, let's go. In the next chapter, we shall look at understanding what romance is.

CHAPTER TWO

Understanding Love And Romance

In this chapter, we take a peek into what love and romance are to understand it better. While jumping headfirst into 'romance mode' is fun and exciting, after a while it will start to become stale just like a relationship can. Being romantic can always be fresh and fun as long and the couple understands what the motives are behind the romance and the underlying intentions. Understanding romance is the most important part of being romantic.

When you decide that you want to begin being romantic, you usually take it slow and carefully consider what your partner likes and prefers when it comes to gifts, actions and gestures. Each romantic expression should have a significant meaning behind it. How you are going to be romantic is far more important that why you are going to be romantic. The process of how you are going to be romantic generally encompasses the 'why' in a much bigger way and is far more effective in conveying any message.

When you first met your spouse, you most likely experienced the 'crush' or 'puppy love' phase of your relationship. While you may experience moments of similar feelings, it is almost impossible to recreate that feeling after spending years together. However, you can always have passion with your spouse. Wouldn't you agree that passion is much more desirable than 'puppy love'?

When you hear people talking about relationships, you often hear them mention the word 'chemistry'. Why is it that people value chemistry with another person over compatibility? If you think about it, compatibility coupled with romance equals passion. Would you prefer basic chemistry or passion in your relationship?

When you look at your partner and you consider being romantic, try not to look too deeply into his or her gender. Gender biasing can really deflate a wonderful intention, especially when it comes to romance. Respect your spouse as the unique individual that he or she is and never allow stereotypes to enter into your romantic intentions. Never point out what you are doing, though! It will be noticed on some level by your spouse. Not only will it be noticed, but it will also be greatly appreciated.

You need to remember that no one is perfect especially when it comes to matters of the heart- this includes romance. You are not and will never be an expert at any point! You will, however, learn and improve as time goes on. Your spouse will teach you through reactions and suggestions as long as you pay attention. It is all worth the time and effort, as life passes by too quickly not to be a hopeless romantic.

No matter how many years you've been living with the same person, you may think that they don't want romance but it's not the case. Everyone wants to have a tremendously rewarding and romantic relationship. It's not an exaggeration to include every single person on the planet. The way in which romance is carried out is usually what makes each relationship unique and sometimes even a challenge! Everything worthwhile takes a little bit of work, but what is more worthwhile than a lasting romance with your spouse? You'll discover that being a romantic makes both of you happier than most other people.

Love is a wonderfully simple concept, but it is never easy. Love and romance work together, hand in hand. Romance is when you show your spouse in your own special way how much you love her without ulterior motives. You introduce romance between you and your partner to show that there is love in your relationship. You express your love through appreciation and in showing him or her that you have been thinking about them and your love. Romance and love is about selfless giving for the pure joy of making your marriage a happy union.

Love can never be expected to be perfect. Although some people might come close to perfect love, it is impossible to achieve. While love is a perfect feeling, humans are imperfect and cannot enjoy the perfection of love without flaws. It doesn't matter, though. Imagine how boring a perfect love would be! Keep in mind that love is never about perfection and it should only be about love. Romance isn't without its imperfections either. You will have hits and misses with romance. What works for one person may not work for another. Romance should simply be about love and it is important to remember that especially when you experience one of those 'misses'.

When it comes to the emotional needs involved with love, men and women tend to far more similar than they are different. When it comes to sex, that's where you'll begin to see the noticeable differences between men and women. Every human being is a complex combination of both physical and psychological characteristics. The closer you move towards the sexual end of things, the noticeable the differences between men and women will be. When you take a look at the emotional needs of both men and women, they become far more similar.

When you approach romance, you cannot approach it as if it is a science or some task that can be controlled or predicted. Romance is an art form that should be expressed as creatively as possible. Romance can be simple or it can be outrageously outrageous! When you enter into a relationship and intend to make romance a strong part of that relationship, you need to make sure that you have an open mind, a creative nature or that you have access to excellent resources that allow you to borrow from other people's creative genius.

Love is something two people have to work at together. You need to be able to set any competitive nature aside and truly enjoy what you are able to give as well as what you receive. If you are always trying to outdo what your spouse has done or even what you have previously done as far as romantic attempts, you will eventually become frustrated and fall flat on your face. That's not very romantic.

Romance should be personal and never feel forced or as if it is part of any bargain. Love should be given freely and accepted freely without conditions or guarantees. Any other expressions of love are doomed to hurt feelings and ultimately failure. In the next chapter, we shall look at why you need to work on your relationship and how you can do that.

CHAPTER THREE

Working On Your Relationship

In this chapter we shall look at how an assessment of where you are in your relationship and why working towards improving your relationship are important. You probably have a good idea of where you and your spouse are in your relationship. If you don't know it, it's probably time to find out. Consider thinking about your relationship, write down where you believe your relationship could use some improvement and talk to your spouse about what you have been thinking and feeling. Achieving an exceptional relationship is not easy, but it is an attainable goal. People who have wonderfully rewarding relationships are loving and giving people. This is a lifestyle that is available to every couple that is willing to work towards such a goal.

When you are looking to have an outstanding relationship with your spouse, you will benefit in more ways than you can imagine. You will be more able to understand you loving relationship in ways that you never thought possible and it helps you to act in ways that satisfy both you and your partner as well as nurture both of you as a couple. An exceptional relationship is one where you and your partner have the best intimate relationship possible, where you are both faithful, passionate, committed to growth, romantic and fascinating, you both consistently work at making your love grow and although not perfect, your relationship is one that you wouldn't trade for anything else in the world.

So, how do you arrive at such an existence with your spouse? You must dedicate yourself to achieving excellence while you work hard, play hard and you both work on your relationship skills together. As simple as it sounds, you both have to live how you love each other each and every day. Great relationships don't just happen. They arise as the result of work,

work, and work! You need to be creative and work together at creating the relationship into one life you can both share together.

Your relationship with your spouse is very individual and only you both know what you want as far as a life together. You are in charge of making your rules and expectations for your individual relationship. This type of direction you can make for your marriage is a wonderful concept in the way people view relationships. You are able to make your relationship into exactly what you want it to be. You are in charge of your goals and in meeting your own standards.

You have the unique knowledge that allows you to create a relationship out of the values you treasure the most like honesty, faith, commitment, creativity, flexibility and equality. With this knowledge as well as the desire to create such a wonderfully romantic and loving desire, you can create a relationship that is not only fulfilling and rewarding but enviable as well.

When you can center your attention on the behaviors in your marriage and not on the personalities, you can focus you attention on setting goals instead of placing blame. This method helps you to set, reach and maintain your goals in order to have the marriage most couples only dream of.

Everyone dreaded report card day in school and if you are dreading making your own relationship report card, then you need to buckle down and study! When you rank all of the aspects of your relationship between you and your spouse, you need to score in the high nineties to achieve an A+. Consider creating a 'relationship report card' with your spouse and watch the awakening you will both experience. When you try to complete your relationship report card, it should not turn into a 'blame game'. It should open the lines of communication and offer some invaluable insight into your relationship as to where you need changes and improvements.

When you consider how you want to grade your partner and yourself, it is a good idea to have some pre-set guidelines as to what each grade means. For example, an 'A' might mean that your partner isn't perfect, but obviously excelling. It could also mean that your partner is loving, attentive, enthusiastic and satisfying. A 'B' could stand for a partner who is always trying, better than most and consistently works on improvement. A 'C' might mean average or acceptable. 'C's' always indicate plenty of room for improvement. 'D's' and 'F's' should be reserved for unhappy situations or even hopeless ones. 'D's' indicate never hopeless while 'F's' require more than just a relationship evaluation. If you find that you and your spouse have areas with a 'D' or an 'F', you need to focus on why you are giving or receiving those grades and commit to some kind of action in order to change and improve that grade. It might involve a commitment on both spouses, but if both are willing to work at it the grade is already moving higher.

When you begin working on your relationship report card, it should be graded the same way your school papers were graded with a number grade (ex. 80%, 50%, 95% and so on). Grade both your partner and yourself in areas like affection, ability to resolve conflict, attitude, commitment, communication skills, consideration level, thinking as a 'couple', creativity, sensitivity, flexibility, generosity, friendship and gift giving skills. Once you've completed that list, continue to evaluate your honesty levels, listening skills, household management skills, patience, love making, romance abilities and practice, playfulness, self-esteem, self-awareness, sense of humor, empathy, tolerance and spontaneity. If you feel that there are any other areas relevant to your particular relationship, feel free to add and evaluate at your discretion.

When you and your spouse are grading each other, be sure to both participate in grading. You can work out your own particulars, but make sure you both have a say in both of your grades. Compare and talk about your grades and why your partner believes you deserve a particular grade (this includes the good grades, too!). You'll be surprised at how your partner sees your relationship and you'll have invaluable insight into how he or she sees your role in the relationship. Just because you may not have earned an A+ in one area doesn't mean that you can't celebrate. Pat yourself (and your partner) on the back for anything over a 'B' and talk about ways you can improve on any 'C's' and 'D's'. The next chapter will look at how having an affair with your spouse is the way to go.

CHAPTER FOUR

Have A Love Affair

In this chapter we shall look at why you should have a love affair - with your spouse. Every marriage is just like any other relationship. There are ups and downs, agreements and disagreements and good days and bad days. When you put two people from different backgrounds with different ideas, feelings and expectations together, you simply can't expect everything to be wonderful all of the time! On a side note, if it is wonderful all the time, there may be an unaddressed set of problems too. While some marriages have very serious problems that can only be solved by intense focus and even therapy, most marriages simply become 'stale' or uninteresting.

It is important to reflect on exactly what is causing any conflict or uneasiness in a marriage before acting on it. In a great many marriages, the excitement and 'take my breath away' feelings are fading or they are even gone. It doesn't mean that the love is gone. When you begin to court your partner first, there is a period of discovery and newness. You find out new things about your partner and your partner discovers new things about you. There is a need to make sure that the other person feels loved. These efforts in the beginning keep the romance alive. After you are married, the newness and the period of discovery give way to stability. By this time, you know almost everything there is to know about your partner and the other way around. In that moment you may begin to feel that the love does not exist anymore. That is however, not true. Love sometimes needs a little stimulation in order to revisit and maintain the feelings we all crave and yearn for. That stimulation is called 'romance.'

Many people mistake a marriage that seems to be ordinary or unexceptional as lacking love. It simply isn't the case! Most marriages do not lack love, but they do lack romance! Love is easy and peaceful, while romance is what makes a relationship hot and arousing.

Every single person on earth in any type of relationship desires passion and romance in his or her life. Unfortunately, there are a few things about romance most people don't understand. The most common problem in creating romance in a relationship is that people simply don't know how to do it! Other times, people are fixed in cultural classifications and their partners are unable to appreciate them for their own special and unique qualities. Ultimately, some people have simply given up on their search for romance.

In a time where everything is convenient and available almost at the touch of a button, the effort of romance seems as if it takes a good deal of effort. It is very possible to take some old-fashioned romantic ideas and make them work in a modern world while maintaining the genuine intention behind each thought and act. Romance today can be filled with unique ideas, creativity and passion. Romance is simply the way you express your love for another person. It is vital to keeping love fresh, exciting and alive. Without romance, love can become tiresome and even worse.

The expression of love through romance keeps it alive, fun and worthwhile. Romance is only true, though, when carried out with no ulterior motives. The only reason romance should be initiated is in an attempt to show love and appreciation. Romance with true intentions is when you want to show your mate that you are thinking about them and they matter enough to make the effort to bring your love to life through action.

Romance is more like an artistic creation as opposed to an exact science. Those who tend to feel competitive in almost everything they do will need to check that attitude at the door when initiating romance. Love and romance should not be considered a contest that should be outdone time and again. It should be considered a cooperative activity. While love and romance take two in order to work, you can be extremely romantic while still keeping your individuality. Love and romance make perfect partners and can make you and your partner 'perfect' companions as well! In the next chapter, we shall look at the impact of thought and action and how both of them are important in a relationship.

CHAPTER FIVE

Thought Vs Action

In this chapter we shall explore the impact of both thought and action on relationships. Consider these two comments - 'It's the thought that counts' and 'Actions speak louder than words'. These two concepts are unique in that they are both true when it comes to any relationship and they also must somehow be balanced well to work properly. Each action or thought truly depends on the two individuals that are involved as well as the particular situation they find themselves in. On the one hand, it is the gesture or the gift that makes an impact while on the other hand it's the thought, the meaning or the intention behind the action that leaves its mark.

Along with the thought and action, there are many other layers involved in what makes any romantic effort in a relationship work or not work. First, it is important to stop stereotyping each other, trying to make assumptions about what he or she thinks, feeling threatened by their position at work, intellectually or otherwise, ignoring feelings and so on. Secondly, it is important to be yourself and accept your partner for who he or she is. Communicate with each other while really listening. Always practice good manners with each other even though you may be comfortable enough to pass wind in front of each other. There is no need to let it all go. Make your relationship your first priority over everything else in your life.

Stop making jokes about male or female behavior or conditions. While it may be funny for the moment, it can become part of how we view each other or how we fear our partner's view us. Don't assume anything that you aren't one hundred percent sure about when it comes to your spouse. He or she will most likely prove you wrong. Don't act as if every action was a huge sacrifice - martyrs can suck a relationship dry. Offer each other trust, hope, the benefit of the doubt and trying to understand how he or she feels before assuming any position.

Sometimes it's best to begin slowly and build up to the more complicated aspects of growing a relationship with anyone. All it takes is one successful step in the right direction and you and your spouse will be hungry for more. Cuddle up together without the television on, the radio on, turn the phones off and if you have kids, put them to bed early. Take him or her to a special tree and carve your initials in together.

Take the time to do something you normally wouldn't do that he or she is sure to enjoy. Men love to have their feet massaged and most women don't know that! Sit him or her down in a chair, place their feet in a hot bin of water, wash and massage their feet, dry them off and go about your day as you normally would!

Try to find a way to provide your love with something he or she can live without but truly enjoys. Does he or she love a white Christmas but you live in an area where snow doesn't fall or the weather isn't cooperating? Find a way to fill your lawn with snow or artificial snow so that you are the one giving them a white Christmas. The more thought you put into the relationship and the more action you translate the thoughts into, the more you will find your relationship thriving. In the next chapter, we shall look at how in a relationship 50 plus 50 is not equal to 100.

CHAPTER SIX

Fifty Plus Fifty Is Not Hundred

In this chapter, we shall see how this simple math equation is wrong in relationships. Everyone knows the old sayings about marriage and how everything requires compromise and each partner should give 50%. Well-they are wrong! Everything should not require compromise or everything will end up turning into a business negotiation and someone will feel that they gave up more than they should have. This leads to resentment and it doesn't have to. While there are certain situations that may be important enough to you or your spouse to make an issue of that will require compromise, it's time to consider making sacrifices here and there for your spouse. He or she will, of course, be surprised when you do so, but they will also begin doing the same for you out of appreciation for you and your actions.

Each partner in a marriage should not be giving 50% all of the time. If you are only giving 50%, you are only doing have as well as you could be doing. If you and your spouse are both giving 100%, you can't go wrong. You are both giving your marriage all of your dedication and effort. If you and your spouse are planning on only meeting each other halfway, you will only be successful half of the time (or maybe even less). Hence, in case of relationships, 100% plus 100% is 100%.

Romance isn't really romance when it's convenient for you or your spouse. Your romantic gestures on romantic days like Valentine's Day or birthdays can only be considered romantic if you go out of your way to be romantic throughout the rest of the year. You don't have to spend money in order to be romantic, either. Begin offering to stop on the way home in case he or she would like you to pick something up. Never allow anyone else to greet him or her at the airport no matter what time the flight arrives. Start getting up and taking care of housework or even the kids before he or she has the chance to ask you to.

Instead of thinking about being romantic, simply do it. Make the decision that you are going to fall in love with your spouse and simply do it. If you spend too much time thinking about it, you will find yourself the victim of self-sabotage. You will focus on faults, hurts and other unimportant distractions that will stop you from reaching your goal. You don't need books or a professional to help you with this process. You simply make the decision and you will do it.

To become more romantic by just doing it, you will find that listening is your best tool. By listening to him or her with more than just your ears - with your eyes and heart as well, you will see that there is so much more to discover about the incredible person you are committed to. Not only will you find that they are offering all sorts of clue and tips on how to be more romantic in your relationship, you will also find opportunities to offer support and fall in love all over again. In the next chapter, we shall look at why it is important to raise the romance another notch when things are going well.

CHAPTER SEVEN

Stepping On The Gas

In this chapter, let us look at how we can step on the gas to raise the romance another notch. It is necessary to go through the beginning steps or 'level 1' of romance in order to move on to bigger and better levels of romance. After you've done all of the traditional things most couples consider to be romantic like chocolates, flowers, jewelry, lingerie, cards, perfume, movies and dinner at fancy restaurants, you are only scratching the surface of the world of romance. While the classics never go out of style, they can become monotonous and lose their novelty. When you are putting effort into being romantic, you will lose your original intent in the monotony of your gestures without growth. If you have a desire for your marriage to endure as well as prosper, you've got to be willing to grow through the romantic process.

Once you have exhausted all of the traditional 'romantic' gestures over a period of time, you no doubt realized that timing had a great deal to with the outcome of any romantic effort. When it comes to romance, timing is crucial. In order to continue growing in the art of romance, you will have to create an element of surprise in order to keep things fresh, exciting, fun and original. In order to create surprises, you will need to work on perfecting your timing.

Timing also has another meaning as your romance grows. You need to pay attention and be sensitive to your partner's involvement at the time of your gift. If he or she is trying to lose weight, then you should never even consider giving him or her chocolate or candy. If he or she is preoccupied with work, they may not have the time to appreciate grand gesture that you worked so hard to plan and you will both end up feeling frustrated and disappointed at the results. Hold on to your big ideas until things are a little less hectic in your lives so that both you and your spouse can savor your romantic efforts.

Once you've moved into more advanced levels of romance, you can do something that is so simply yet should be very well received. Whenever you go to a party or other social event, flirt with him or her just a little bit. Once you've done this a few times, pretend you are living out a 'pick-up' fantasy with him or her but don't let any of the other guests know what is going on. Continue with your fantasy all the way home (giggling is allow, but don't let it spoil the mood!).

At the next social gathering, 'pick him or her up' again, but continue with the fantasy at the party. While you are at the party, sneak off together to have wild, passionate sex. You will both probably talk about that night for some time to come! (Especially if you get caught, so remember to lock the door!) Once you've completed your romantic wooing, take a break for a while before starting again. Imagine the build of anticipation for the climax (pun is intended) of your game. In the next chapter, we shall look at the attitude of romance.

CHAPTER EIGHT

The Attitude Of Romance

In this chapter, we shall look at understanding the attitude of romance. It might seem quite exciting to have all kinds of romantic ideas and suggestions floating through your head at this point, but it is important to remember that romance can't be rushed or piled on all at once. If it is, all of the intentions behind every move will be lost or misinterpreted. It is important to keep in mind that romance is best when you don't misrepresent yourself or who you are to your spouse, you always start with the basics and you move forward a single step at a time.

If you change your mental attitude so that you can commit yourself to creating romance in your marriage, you can make just about anything romantic. As difficult as it might seem, with the right mindset you can make cleaning the toilet a romantic task. On the other hand, without a committed romantic attitude, you can take a beautiful stroll on a moonlit beach and turn it into an unhappy and uncomfortable experience.

You must have some sort of feelings for your spouse or you wouldn't be interested in improving your marriage by adding romance. Romance is simply about taking action on how you feel towards your spouse. Because love is a feeling, your spouse can't see the proof in the emotion because it is something that isn't tangible and can be seen or touched. You feel the love for your spouse and the romance is the action that comes about as a result of that love. Romance will start as a new attitude with the right intentions, but it must grow beyond. It must be able to *show* your spouse how much you love him or her through actions in words, presents, gentle caresses and more.

Once you become a beginning romantic and you are well into your romantic thought processes, you will find that your spouse is truly appreciative of all the little things that you do for him or her. It's the small things you've added to your daily lives like making sure he or she knows their loved before anything else is said or the phone call for no particular reason other than to tell them that they are on your mind. These small actions tend to stay with the other person longer and have more of an impact than expensive, materialistic gifts.

Most marriages suffer from a bland and generic form of romance born of obligation. These couples honor Valentine's Day, birthdays and anniversaries only because it is necessary if they want to be able to sleep in their own bed that night. Special marriages that others find enviable take advantage of a rare form of romance that is practiced as more of an option than an obligation. These couples choose to be romantic not because they have to, but because they want to. While they still honor the 'obligatory' special days, all of the other days are just as special because they have made them that way with each other. In the next chapter, we shall look at the need to pay attention to the cues we get from our partners.

CHAPTER NINE

Pay Attention

In this chapter, we shall learn the importance of paying attention to cues from our partners as an effective way of keeping romance alive. Remember when you were young, free and looked for ways to have fun with your friends and spouse? Over the years, we often find it difficult to stay young at heart when life overwhelms us with responsibility, stress and even consuming worries about financial or employment concerns. We no longer look for the fun in anything. In fact, sometimes others attempting to have fun can irritate us even further! Well, it needs to stop right now. You're being far too grown up and sucking the fun right out of your life and your spouse's life as well. It's time to re-connect with your inner child and extend the offer to find fun again to your spouse.

Think back to when you and your spouse were dating and try to remember the most fun you two had together. Start remembering together by doing it all over again right now! Take this idea a step further by trying to remember the most fun you've ever had while your clothes were on and, of course, then try to remember the most fun you've ever had while your clothes were off! Do them both again! And do them again if you want to!

When you live with someone and you want to have fun with them, it is essential that you pay attention to what they like and what they don't like. If you are the only one having fun because you've stepped on his or her toes or feelings, there really isn't any fun being had. For example, we all have certain things that make us angry or what some call "hot topics". Learn what your spouse's hot topics are and try not to bring them up. You as well as your spouse also have certain actions that irritate you or "pet peeves". Again, learn them and try avoiding them!

Your spouse also has a number of things from which they derive pleasure. Your spouse, no matter how composed he or she may be, has areas of emotional vulnerability. Learn what they are and indulge those areas.

Also, pay attention to what turns your partner on and rehearse, practice, rehearse, practice and so on! It is also important to know what your spouse considers to be a 'turn off' so that you can avoid doing so. If you do something that turns your partner off, it could undo all of the 'turning on' you've been working so hard at.

Keep in mind that there are endless ways that you can express love to your spouse and when you add fun into the mix, it can become a lasting memory. Always accept your partner's reactions and responses as honest expressions of their love even though it might not be what you had hoped for or anticipated. This is part of accepting your partner for who he or she is and learning to see past your own disappointment or insecurities. If you have difficulty with the way you are viewing his or her attempt at romance, you might simply begin a conversation about his or her needs while contributing your own thoughts and feelings. If you work with your partner instead of conflicting with him or her, you will both be much happier and your romance with grow much quicker. In the next chapter, we shall see how we end up rationalizing the absence of romance in our lives.

CHAPTER TEN

Rationalization For No Romance

In this chapter, we shall look at how rationalization of the absence of romance in our lives kills a relationship. So many relationships come in second, third or even worse to the many distractions in our daily lives. Unfortunately, these distractions are allowing too many marriages to end in divorce or a couple simply co-exists for years longing for happiness and fulfilment. It simply doesn't have to be this way. It's time to take a look at what is really important and what will matter in the long run. Once your job or other commitments are gone, all you'll have left is an empty marriage or an empty home to face every day. It's time to stop making excuses and find the time to romance your spouse starting today.

Some women truly believe that some men aren't genetically capable of being romantic. No matter how masculine a guy is, he is capable of romance! It is just another excuse for people to let their relationship slide. Romance leads to happy relationships while relationships without romance lead to loneliness or even worse. All men are and can show that they are romantic. So can all women.

When you envision romance, you probably think about a great deal of materialistic exchanging happening between you and your spouse. Romance isn't about what is tangible or how much you spent. Romance is about the thought and intention behind every gesture you make. As long as the thought is behind your efforts, you will have romance. Improving your relationship with better companionship, sex and attention is very romantic alone!

If you've decided to be romantic, you have one chance to forget about your commitment. Just one chance and then that's it. From then on it's an excuse- a bad one at that- and you will do more damage to your relationship than you thought possible from neglecting your spouse. If you are constantly forgetting, you are displaying behavior that can only be interpreted as your spouse simply isn't that important to you.

Procrastination is the archenemy of romance. While your career is and should be important, your spouse should be more important. Imagine sitting on your front porch in your golden years while looking back at everything you've accomplished as well as any regrets you might have. Do you really thing you'll be wishing you had spent more time working?

For the belligerent spouses out there, its most likely crossed you mind that you don't have to be romantic because you shouldn't have to prove your love to your spouse. Being married and bringing romance into your relationship isn't about proving anything. Romance with your spouse is about showing how much you appreciate and love him or her.

Don't drag your heels when it comes to being romantic. Putting it off can become just as bad as never ever doing it at all and the habit is quite easy to fall into. Consider the fact that you don't know how long you and your spouse will be lucky enough to have each other. Whether he or she will become deceased or they leave your procrastinating butt, you simply don't have the time to put off making your marriage and incredibly loving and romantic partnership. That said, in the next chapter, we shall take a look at some basic rules and regulations governing romance.

CHAPTER ELEVEN

Romance Regulations

In this chapter, let us look at some rules and regulations to make romance work. You know that you want to make your relationship with your spouse special and romance is the ideal way to do that. Romance keeps the passion and love alive in any relationship, but just like most good things romance comes with a few rules in order to make it work. Romance can be planned or spontaneous and both are perfectly acceptable. Spontaneous romance is almost always wonderful because both you and your spouse are often caught up in the moment and you are both sharing an intimate experience together. It is often when you plan romance that mistakes can be made if you aren't aware of the rules of romance.

The first and probably most important rule of romance is that your relationship should always come first in your life. While this may be a difficult concept for those who have put so much time and effort into your career, but when you are retired and cuddling with your spouse on the front porch you probably won't be wishing you had spent more time at work. Everything in your life should be an outpouring from your relationship. Everything you do should be because of your marriage and the love you share with your spouse. When considering this idea, be sure not to mistake it with being the one in your relationship who must always suffer for the sake of principle. That can only hurt your relationship. A good marriage consists of two people who always support and encourage each other.

When you bring romance into your relationship, it is crucial that you understand it is your spouse who defines what is romantic. You can give her chocolates, flowers and jewelry until you are broke, but it won't do a thing for your marriage if she doesn't like chocolate, flowers and jewelry. The same goes for wives giving to husbands. Pay attention to his or her likes and dislikes. There's no point in cooking a special meal all day long if he's got a craving for chicken wings.

When two people get married and their lives grow together, there seems to be less and less opportunity for spontaneity. This isn't a bad thing! Planning is simply creating the opportunity. Plan out a week or even an entire month of romance. Plan your Anniversary celebration. Plan a surprise night out on the town. The element of surprise is just as good as spontaneity. In fact, it's probably better. You spent time putting thought and effort into your gesture. Impulsive is great, but planned can be better.

Romance doesn't always mean presenting gifts. Gifts are wonderful gestures, especially if they are something he or she can truly appreciate but they cannot compensate for some of the more important romantic gestures in a relationship- special time with each other. Special time with each other doesn't mean going out and doing things each weekend. Spending times together on the sofa or not rushing through dinner and enjoy each other's company is very romantic.

Romance is sort of like a wonderful way in which people can balance each other. This can come about in a lot of different ways that are probably already occurring in your relationship. You simply don't know how to see it yet. Think about what has changed about your since you married your spouse. You can probably say that quite a bit has changed. Now think about how much hasn't changed since you got married. You can probably say that quite a bit hasn't changed as well. Your spouse, your love and your romance offer the opportunity to balance your relationship beautifully.

You may feel threatened in some way when you think about surrendering completely to your love for your spouse. Remember that you can always lose yourself in that love without risking losing your individuality. You can also allow yourself and even embrace change without losing what it is about you that makes you unique. Compromise is always possible without having to compromise who you are. Growth is always possible and it never has to mean growing apart. You and your spouse are capable of having disagreements without arguments. You can allow yourself to experience emotion and feelings without losing control of yourself.

Trust is essential in any relationship- especially a marriage. You can give in to your partner without the fear of losing anything. You can open up to him or her without the fear of being judged. It is possible to keep the passion alive in your marriage for the duration of your lifetime, you can remain a responsible adult while indulging in your inner child and the only time you are truly known is in your intimate, long-term relationship- your marriage.

Your lover cannot know who you truly are unless you open up your heart completely. You cannot be a participant in a loving relationship without being vulnerable. Being intimate always comes with a risk even if you are with your spouse and you must be willing to face that risk.

Both you and your spouse need to make sure that you create a supportive environment or else you will never be able to share your feelings freely with each other. Spontaneity and control don't work well together. In fact, they can't work together at all. If control is an issue for either you and/or your spouse, it needs to be addressed. You will never be able to be interdependent with your spouse unless you are first able to be independent on your own. Dependence is a harmful thing in any relationship and it must be changed into a healthy dependence.

Both spouses need to be open to the fact that neither of you can grow without learning from your mistakes. Once you learn how to forgive yourself, you can learn how to forgive others and grudges cannot be held. Broken hearts will not heal unless that heart is put at risk again.

The point of romance is to grow together in love and intimacy. Love and intimacy can mean a number of different things to different people and all of them are essential to a healthy relationship. Live together, learn together, grow together and love together. In the next chapter, we shall look at some of the mistakes made in relationships.

CHAPTER TWELVE

Mistakes In Romance

In this chapter, we shall look at some of the common mistakes in romance. Being romantic is wonderful, fun and especially rewarding but unfortunately, many people make mistakes we all make in relationships that can simply undo all of the good that has been done by romantic efforts. For instance, every couple has disagreements and upon occasion the argument has a definitive outcome. The spouse that was right during the argument has two choices when 'winning'- he or she cannot see it as winning and simply move on or express understanding as to why there may have been some confusion. Or, he or she can gloat and make their spouse feel inferior and possibly humiliated. One works (the moving on one...) and one doesn't (the gloating one).

Conflict is often unavoidable when two people from two different backgrounds with different beliefs are brought together. If you happen to be the one in a disagreement who doesn't come out as the 'right' one or you don't get your way, the worst thing you can do is to pout. It's simply childish, not sexy at all and your partner will most likely have a difficult time finding respect for you as a result.

While worry is a natural part of life, try not to let it overwhelm your relationship. Wouldn't you rather focus on much more positive things like romance? If you find that you and your spouse schedule a lot during the week, sit down and try to eliminate some commitments. Don't over-schedule any time that you don't have to, including vacations and weekends.

Make choices that benefit both you and your spouse. Instead of turning on the television, ask your wife or husband if they would like to play a board game or go for a walk. If you decide to watch television together, never guess at the plot or give away the ending of a movie! Try to support your spouse's authority in front of the children. If you disagree about what was done, wait until you can talk quietly with your spouse and discuss why and how things may have been done differently. He or she can always go back and change their mind or you may eventually come to support his or her decisions.

Make as much as possible in your relationship about 'us' instead of about 'you'. This doesn't mean that you or your spouse has to sacrifice his or her individuality, it simply means that all decisions and thoughts about the relationship should be about both needs instead of your own individual needs. For instance, if you happen to be or sleep with someone who 'hogs' the bed covers go out and find an extra, extra large blanket so that there's plenty for both to share. Don't make an issue out of it- make a joke and provide a solution.

Show your spouse that you are a loving and mature individual by doing mature and loving things like never holding grudges or continuously bringing up errors from the past. You can also be a good listener, never interrupt and wait your turn. And most importantly, don't allow a day to pass by without telling your spouse that you love them.

Another unfortunate habit some couples have come to rely on is a 'romance exchange', which isn't true romance. What this refers to is when a couple has an argument, disagreement or conflict of any kind, one will often present the other with a gift or token as a sort of apology. While this has the appearance of being 'romance', it really isn't when you are using your gesture as an exchange for forgiveness. It is also absolutely not romantic or just plain right to become 'romantic' in order to bargain for favors you want. For example, bringing home flowers and takeout should not lead you to expect sex that night. Bringing home flowers and dinner should be a gesture of love and because you want to show your appreciation for your spouse. Expecting something in return is asking for a payoff for you actions.

In addition to the 'romance exchange', there are a number of things that simply don't qualify as romantic gestures. These situations and gifts could easily be referred to as the 'never exchange' list! First of all never let anything distract you when you are having a conversation with your spouse. Ignore the call waiting (let the voice mail pick it up), turn off the TV (don't just mute it) or order the kids to leave you alone in your bedroom while you talk. It doesn't even have to be a serious or important discussion. Every couple needs to have their own time to communicate in order to make each other feel respected and understood.

Other 'nevers' to be kept in mind include never do home improvement projects where tension is bound to be a factor (like wallpapering), don't ever do anything that will embarrass the other person in public, never show a lack of respect for your partner and always keep each other's secrets. Respect is a huge part of any relationship and should always be honored in every way. Never take the liberty of throwing something away that belongs to your spouse. Make sure you ask first and respect their response. Never give your spouse a gift that most would consider 'practical' unless you are absolutely sure it will knock his or her socks off (some guys just can't get enough power tools).

When living with a spouse, there are a number of things that we can do that can hurt the other person without even realizing the pain we have caused. Never use the old, "yes, dear" phrase in order to pacify him or her. Let her have her PMS time during the month without having to deal with jokes or anger about the condition. It is a real medical condition and during PMS is the worst time to even think about taking about it! Never, ever withhold sex in order to get what you want or to punish your spouse. Both husbands and wives have been known to participate in this practice and it is incredibly harmful to the trust and respect in any relationship.

The obvious 'nevers' in any relationship include never forgetting birthdays, anniversaries and Valentine's Day. Always remember to say "I love you" before moving on to more pressing matters like what's for dinner. In the next chapter, we shall look at embracing the imperfection in your partner.

CHAPTER THIRTEEN

Embrace The Differences

In this chapter, we shall see why embracing the differences between you and your partner is the way to go. We've all heard the expression that 'opposites attract'. Heck, even Paula Abdul made a song dedicated to such a phenomenon. While opposites can seem to have the biggest challenges ahead of them when they get married, they also have to most opportunities for love and romance. People who embrace romance and actually admit that they enjoy romance are more likely to be successfully married to their opposite. It just goes to show you how powerful romance can be in any marriage!

There is a very famous book available at any bookstore, online book retailer or your local library that is worth a look at some point. It is called *Men are From Mars and Women are From Venus* by John Gray. The book is a wonderful attempt to explain the natural differences between men and women. The author's point in his book is to basically help men and women to acknowledge, understand and accept these differences before they can move on and enjoy fuller, happier relationships. Mr. Gray offers a spirited look at these differences that are intended to explain these differences so that men and women might be able to adjust their thinking so that they find it easier to understand intentions and meaning behind thought processes and actions.

The first step in understanding the differences between men and women is to acknowledge that there are, in fact, differences between the sexes especially in the way that they communicate with each other. Men simply do not think the way that women do and women simply do not think the way that men do. For example, if a woman declares that she would like to go out to dinner and a movie her husband would most likely not think of her idea as a romantic one. He is more likely to immediately think about how much a night out will cost and become stressed about it. When a man gives a woman risqué lingerie, he is thinking about how wonderful she will look in it. A woman is more likely to think that he is trying to get her to look like a prostitute. The use of the word romance can be quite slippery as well with a woman using romance to refer to love while a man usually infers sex when he refers to romance. Be careful and clarify intentions before things go too far.

When you are buying lingerie for your husband, keep in mind that it is for *him*. You are buying it to thrill and to please him. Choose colors that you know *he* will like. Studies show that while women prefer pastel colored lingerie, men prefer to see their women in red and black lingerie. Make sure that the lingerie is truly chose for your spouse and not just what makes you happy.

Women have a natural habit of complaining that is and has been referred to for decades as 'nagging'. Women need to stop nagging, no matter what the cause of the nag. Men tend to be quite judgmental. Women do not want to be judged or corrected. They also resent any type of conversation that resembles a lecture. She doesn't want or need it and will end up resenting you for it.

Instead of focusing on the conflict of nature between men and women, focus on the wonderful attributes each partner has to bring into the relationship. Talk more, listen better and make fewer assumptions. Also, try to appreciate your spouse for more than just his or her differences. Appreciate him or her for the good that they bring to your marriage.

Every marriage experiences problems and even misunderstandings from small tiffs to shouting matches and the reason for this is often because both spouses are not able to acknowledge, recognize and appreciate their differences or the principle of balancing opposites. Everything is intended to be able to work with and often balance its opposite. Life is full of opposites that complement each other like man and woman, happy and sad, funny and serious, give and take as well as life and death.

Opposites offer insight into the magic of how life is balanced. If you begin to see your spouse as your equivalent on the opposite side of the scale of life, you should find that you have a new appreciation for his or her individuality.

Try seeing everything you experience in your marriage at complementary experiences or behaviors. For instance, instead of using your differences with your spouse as a reason for conflict, try considering them as an important part of the person you love and celebrate them. While the opposite traits may seem to stand out, you undoubtedly have some common traits you share with your spouse. Find strength with your spouse because of your similarities.

Take each day with your spouse and live it to the fullest. At the same time, it is a wonderful idea to make your memories a part of what makes your romance special. If you love reading books, buy some more but make them about something that your spouse is interested in. He or she may never read the book, but you will have and you can share all kinds of thoughts and ideas that you may not have been able to before. At the same time, stop relying on books that tell you how to improve your marriage. You already have all that you need without them. You and your spouse are already there!

Make sure you aren't holding anything back in your relationship. Each partnership tends to have an individual who would rather bury their feelings than express them and possibly cause conflict or wounded feelings. It is absolutely all right to express how you feel as long as your words are chosen carefully. Never take on an accusative tone and always make sure you emphasize what you are saying is how you *feel*.

You are married to your best friend. If you don't treat him or her like they are your best friend already, it's time to start right now. On the other hand, sometimes it might be fun to act like he or she is a stranger to spice things up. Imagine a chance to get to know one another all over again! In the next chapter, we shall look at acknowledging the similarities, despite the differences.

CHAPTER FOURTEEN

Acknowledge The Similarities

In this chapter, we read about how despite the differences there are also similarities that we can learn to acknowledge and appreciate. While there is no arguing that men and women have very real differences, it doesn't give you an excuse to ignore all of the wonderful similarities men and women share. For example, love is not an emotion owned or mastered by a single sex. Love is for both sexes to experience, share and enjoy. If love is not for a single sex, then neither is romance. Romance is for both men and women. In fact, romance cannot work without the two sexes working together at it. Men and women may have different ways of thinking and reacting, but underneath it all men and women both have the same needs.

Relationships and traditional gender roles have change drastically over the past century. While a wife would once never consider sending her husband flowers at work, it is a common gesture today. In fact, most men would feel comfortable and flattered if they were to receive flowers at work. Flowers are also appreciated when delivered to the home. Women tend to have a hard time thinking about men as romantic and sentimental beings. They should keep in mind that a man wrote one of the greatest love stories of all time in *Romeo and Juliet*. Nicholas Sparks is one of the most romantic authors of today and he, too, is a man. Some of the most talented dancers with the lightest feet have been men like Gene Kelly and Fred Astaire.

Try and look at any differences between you and your spouse as personality differences instead of differences between the sexes. While it is easy to lump both men and women into gender-specific categories, it would be unfair and completely inaccurate. Not all women are sensitive and emotion. Not all men are aggressive and logical. While these thoughts might seem to be generally true, the special and unique qualities in your particular spouse are the reason why you fell in love with him or her in the first place.

Try to sit down in a quiet and private place with your spouse. Talk about how and why you fell in love with him or her. Offer him or her the opportunity to do the same for you. The only rule is that both of you have to be very, very specific. Make a mental note of how many qualities are gender-specific and how many are not. You might find yourself surprised at the results. Your next job is to keep in mind your own answers and work at supporting and enjoying those qualities in your partner on a daily basis.

The key to recognizing differences between you and your spouse is to not focus on them. If you focus on them or place too much emphasis on them, you will create conflict that needn't be there. Look at what that particular quality brings to the relationship or how is can be a positive influence. Use romance to connect you as lovers and spouses as well as a tool to accept and appreciate each other's differences. Let us bust some relationship and romance myths in the next chapter.

CHAPTER FIFTEEN

Busting A Few Myths

The institution of marriage is surrounded by a number of myths, stories and advice freely offered by people on a daily basis. Unfortunately, many people listen to and believe these pieces of so-called wisdom to the point where it doesn't help their marriage and it only hinders its growth. Many of the myths regarding relationships are incredibly damaging and it is unfortunate that they are such common beliefs. Once you understand why certain bits of advice or information can be regarded as myths, you can break through what could be blocking the growth of your marriage. In fact, you may actually learn to appreciate your spouse and your role in your marriage even more.

Sometimes holding on to the myths and old-fashioned views of relationships and marriage are all that hold couples back from having a truly wonderfully fulfilling and happy relationship. It is important to recognize your spouse and his or her own special individual with so much to offer you and your relationship if you love, support and respect your partner. Encouraging your partner through support, understanding and appreciation are crucial to breaking through stereotypes and the myths that surround relationships between men and women. Working through and dismissing that type of information as old-fashioned, irrelevant and flat-out wrong can open doors in your marriage you didn't even know were closed.

When things become tense between you and your partner, keep in mind some of the stereotypes you might be clinging to and work to dispel them from your psyche. For example, if one of you or both of you believe that romance is the best way to hide or disguise your faults, it simply isn't the case. Someone who is not a nice person doesn't miraculously change because they present their spouse with flowers. That spouse still isn't a nice person. Romantic gestures may disguise some faults for a short time, but a person's true self always come through. If you are realistic about who you are and your expectations of each other, then romance can work wonders to improve your relationship.

If you give them an inch, they'll take a mile and if you married them you most likely would have seen it by now. There isn't any truth to this particular saying and it only sets us up to be suspicious of someone who really hasn't done anything in order to earn our suspicion. If you give a little bit consistently, you will be satisfying your partner and they won't need that extra. If you don't ever give or give so infrequently that your efforts are forgotten, your spouse has every right to demand a mile from you. Give him or her an inch and enjoy the journey down the rest of the mile together.

Nice guys finish last is one of the worst possible sayings floating around today. Whoever thought of that and actually uttered those words must have been feeling truly low and full of self-pity because there simply cannot be any other explanation. Nice guys never finish last. They may have a longer and harder road sometimes, but it isn't often that you see the bullies and jerks finishing first. If they aren't, who is? It's the nice guys, but they are so nice and gracious you don't hear them bragging about it. It is also important to note that the word 'nice' doesn't mean 'weak' or 'effeminate' in any way. Nice means socially or conventionally correct; refined or virtuous and not at all negative in any way. Nice is not another word for push over or spineless. Nice is as close to a 'perfect' man as you can come and they always end up first in line.

Romance is all you need in order to save your relationship is a wonderfully optimistic thought, but not quite accurate. If simple romance were enough to save a marriage, it would be running wonderfully rampant throughout the world today. Unfortunately, it takes more than simple romance. If you truly feel love for your spouse and you are expressing it through romance, then it will save your marriage. If you are trying to use romance to buy some time or to placate your spouse, then you are only buying time or placating your spouse. Your time as a married couple is most likely limited and should be attended to immediately by a professional.

If you think that once you marry someone that you can change him or her, you are in for a rude awakening. You cannot change a person, yet you can make an impact on how they may see things, you can help them adjust to new or unfamiliar ways of thinking and you can always resort to manipulation, but nothing will change or even fix your spouse. Never manipulate or push your partner into a direction he or she resists. You may be the one who needs to alter your way of thinking or viewing things.

You may be able to do that on your own or require the help of a therapist in order to show you the skills you need for better understanding and acceptance of you and your spouse. If you feel there are problems between you and your spouse due to personality conflicts, try working together to learn how to express thoughts and feelings better and more productively. If you are both in love, you will find the romance in there somewhere.

Sensationalist television, magazines and talk radio have been key players when it comes to fueling any belief that there is a battle between the sexes happening. While there are definitively some physical and psychological differences, they are not enough to earn the term 'battle' as a description. When you allow yourself to consider any kind of battle between the sexes, you risk grouping all men or all women into a certain category and that leads to stereotyping. Once you recognize that your partner is a unique individual with a number of positive attributes, you can shed the thought that there should be any type of conflict between the two of you. Any thought of battle or conflict only leads to lack of communication, misunderstandings and discourages growth in any relationship. The last chapter in this section will focus on some truths about romance and relationships that you always knew but needed to hear from someone.

CHAPTER SIXTEEN

Truths You Need To Hear

In this chapter, we shall explore a few well-known facts that you may already know but may have forgotten.

Relationships are never always easy. It is normal to hit some bumps in the road or to even have long stretches where you and your partner have a hard time connecting. Couples who are lucky enough to seem to get along more often than not have probably discovered a little secret early on in their marriage. That secret is to show love and affection in little ways often- not always in big ways when things seem to be going badly or when an apology is in order!

One of the best ways to be successful in any relationship is to have fun! Sometimes it might feel a little bit awkward, but once you remember how good it feels to act like a kid, sweet, silly and just plain carefree, you will find you prefer it to your adult life! Make sure you revisit and care for your 'inner child'. This is the part of you that can unlock all of your creativity, spontaneity, feeling of wonder and happiness. Take this part of you and make it a part of your relationship. While there are always times when you have to be an adult, there are also times when it is absolutely fine to be wonderfully carefree and joyful!

Has timing always been an issue for you no matter what you try to do? Maybe you're someone who can be creative, but you're not sure when would be the perfect time to surprise your husband or wife. Timing can be crucial depending on the sort of romance you have in mind with your spouse. Sometimes you must plan romance while other times you have to always keep a watchful eye out for the right moment to present itself. You might think you are blind to those moments or you simply don't have any instinct for timing, but here are a few ideas to get you started and hopefully find your own groove.

Although being creative might be something you don't think you have within you, you simply haven't found a way to tap into your creative potential. While you may not know where your particular strengths lie, you can discover what works for you and your spouse as well as what doesn't work with a few simple ideas to get you started.

The best thing about romance in a relationship is that it is shared. While one partner may initiate it, both end up enjoying any romantic effort. Romance is a relationship activity and cannot work if both partners aren't participants. When you decide that romance is the way you want to go in order to improve your marriage or even work towards having an outstanding marriage, start planning your romance in advance with both you and your partner in mind. Even if you are giving a gift to your partner, keep in mind how it will affect you when you present it to him or her. Some gifts are actually meant for both of you although it is presented to only one partner (ex. Massage oil). Both of you must enjoy the romance in order for it to be effective in your relationship.

Every marriage experiences spouses buying gifts for one another. Most of the time the gifts are for what are considered to be 'mandatory' gift giving days like birthdays, anniversaries, Christmas and so on. Sometimes spouses use gifts as gestures to say that they are sorry or to earn forgiveness. These aren't gifts at all- they are bribes and they don't serve any purpose other than to be a Band Aid to wounds that require proper attention to heal.

The best gifts given in any relationship are gifts that have only one intention and that intention is to let your spouse know that you are thinking of them, appreciate them and love them. These gifts are given without ulterior motives or expectations. These gifts only work when they are chosen with a great deal of thought, care and without anticipating anything in return.

As with any romantic gesture, don't overdo the gift giving. If he or she receives gifts all of the time, it isn't special. Pace yourself, put thought into everything you do and always consider your spouse before taking any action. While jewelry is typically considered a gift for women, the girls can pay attention to these suggestions for special adornments intended for their husbands. If you are buying jewelry that is intended to last a lifetime, you are most likely going to spend a good deal of money on a single piece. In order to make sure you are getting your money's worth, you should know more about what you are buying.

If you are spending time looking for ways in which you can improve your relationship, you obviously love and care for your partner and what you want to have together. Start your changes by celebrating your relationship! Celebrate the joy of having met that one very special person, find joy in the wonderful things that 'click' about you and your spouse and celebrate what you are committed to building together. You can celebrate any day at any time and you can also celebrate by surprising your spouse.

While the traditional romantic gestures may be fine for some, others don't feel comfortable following in other people's shoes. Maybe they've already done all of the traditional romantic things they can think of and it's becoming tiresome for both spouses. Luckily, there are a number of new ideas that can be derived from old ones. Instead of thinking about the same old things you've always done, consider honoring a tradition by giving it a new twist or simply make some changes. Not only can you change what you would normally do for a holiday or special occasion, but you can also change some of your existing daily habits to turn your marriage into a 24/7-romance wheel.

While most people acknowledge that opposites attract, they are also quick to point out the men and women generally tend to be different in a number of ways. Although this is basically true, it isn't an excuse to not have romance in your marriage. Men and women can both be romantic with their spouse once they understand the likes and dislikes of their partner. Sometimes it just takes a little patience, attention and effort on your part to get things going and to make romance happen.

Some couples are genuinely motivated when it comes to creativity and romance. Others take a little prompting and pushing. For those who want to be hopeless romantics but work better when they have a simple guide to work by, there are romance orders that can only lead you to your own couple's romance cure. Follow these steps and you might just find that you actually enjoy some of your own ideas that spontaneously pop into you head!

Relationships take work, work and more work, but it takes *hard* work to have a successful, happy and fulfilling relationship. While you may feel like you are working very hard at your relationship, you need to work harder. You can never put enough effort into making a relationship successful. After the initial 'work' it may not seem so much like work once you've introduced or stepped up romance into your marriage. For those of you who feel that you are hitting a brick wall when it comes to being creatively romantic in your relationship, here are a few ideas to get you going.

When you got married, you said the words of commitment we all know so well about for better or worse, for richer or for poorer and so on. Those words are wonderfully inspiring, but real life sometimes make those vows seem as if they are mocking couples after they've been married for several years. The vows aren't the problem because they are simply defining true commitment. What becomes difficult is keeping the love and romance alive in a marriage.

If you can think back to the first year you and your spouse were dating (or weeks for some!) before getting married, try and recall how overwhelming that feeling of love was for that person. When you remember, try to think about doing something so huge that it reflects the amount of love you once felt and continue to feel for your spouse.

When thinking about what you can do to express how you feel towards your spouse, think as big as you can while considering financial restrictions. You won't need to use baby steps when trying to be romantic. When it comes to showing your love and commitment in any marriage, bigger is ALWAYS better.

You don't have to be dramatic or especially outrageous in order to pull off a big, loving gesture for your spouse. Even the most reserved and quiet person can find it in them to put a banner together or cut some cardboard for the one that they love. Many people who have already enjoyed the results of their efforts proudly display their "big" romantic gift permanently in their home or they placed it securely in a safe place.

Romance is all around you. You simply have to know where to begin looking for it! With a society filled with instant food, instant messaging and instant results, it's difficult to think about having to actually do something on your own without assistance. Romance is work without the assistance of a computer or other electronic device that can make it easier on you. When you are dealing with romance, you are working on a relationship with another human being and one-on-one attention and contact cannot be substituted. Your mission to accept as one of the newest hopeless romantics is to truly listen to your spouse. You aren't just listening to him or her, though. You are really hearing what they are saying to you. He or she is your greatest romantic idea resource available and you can move on to other resources from there.

Open up the reception in your ears to a whole new way of discovering your spouse through interests and romance. Don't discount anything and never stop listening. Your discovery and learning process should never end!

You are never too old to play games. Well, there are some games you shouldn't be playing at this point in your relationship. You shouldn't be playing on his or her guilt and you shouldn't be manipulating in order to get what you want. Those games are unacceptable, inappropriate and they will only serve to deteriorate any trust and respect that might exist in your marriage. The kind of games I'm talking about includes having fun with each other. You can have fun with each other every single day you are married! Fun only takes a moment or you can take much longer if you have the time. Fun and love go hand in hand as well as allow a partnership to grow in laughter and trust.

You and your spouse seem to be searching for something that is missing in your relationship. While you know that there aren't huge issues that should be dealt with in therapy or counseling, you simply can't put your finger on why things seem so dull and unexciting. Sometimes you even question whether or not you are both 'in love' anymore. You feel almost desperate and improving your situation seems hopeless. It's not hopeless! You need a little help in how to begin appreciating each other again through small gestures and thoughtful intentions called romance.

Whether you consider yourself together or 'two-gether', you will both find a wonderfully comforting yet exciting familiarity with each other. Familiarity never truly spawns into contempt, as the saying goes. Relationships that exist without creativity and satisfaction are the kinds that spawn contempt. Doing things together with your spouse doesn't mean that you become dependent on each other. Dependence is absolutely the worst thing for your relationship and will ultimately lead to an unhealthy co-dependency. Complete independence is not altogether good for a marriage either. If you are so focused on your own independence, you can never be a true *couple*. Interdependence is what almost all successful couples have been able to achieve and maintain. Interdependence is simply a reciprocal relation between interdependent individuals. It is possible to achieve such a balance in a relationship and it is the best way to have a respectful and successful partnership with your spouse.

If you've made the efforts to complete an entire week of romance with your spouse, you may or may not have been able to come up with your own ideas. If you find that you haven't been bit with the romance inspiration bug on your own, you can plan several weeks of romance for you and your spouse with a few more suggestions. Once you've implemented the ideas that work for you and you've been doing them for a while, you are sure to be inspired with your own thoughts and ideas.

Sometimes spontaneity is something that some people aren't used and they avoid it because they fear that it may cause quite a shock to their system. If you feel like you aren't ready to spring the romance on your spouse or it might work better for your marriage to approach romance in a more organized fashion, you can actually schedule romance into your week. This method of romance introduction also works well with people who feel that they are too busy to bother with spontaneous romance. You most likely already have your calendar loaded with commitments and reminders, so your romantic schedule should work out quite well with your particular type of lifestyle.

Almost every love story has the potential to begin as if it were a fairy tale. "Once upon a time, two people fell passionately in love and their love was unlike any others before theirs." Relationship beginnings are wonderful and they can experience a 'rebirth' with a wedding, honeymoon and the exciting first year of marriage. Once a couple begins to grow and their lives change with jobs, children, social activities and other commitments, the love and romance becomes more difficult to attend to. Sometimes love and romance seem to be lost altogether. This destiny is not unavoidable if you want to rekindle the passion or simply bring it to a new level by becoming a hopeless romantic.

When you want to ignite the passion in your relationship but you aren't sure what you need to do, the best place to begin is at the beginning. Think about the things that you used to do for your partner at the beginning of your relationship. If you don't remember or never tried to be a true romantic, don't worry. It's not difficult and once you begin you will find that you will get your own new ideas after a while.

Are you in the mood for love? Maybe you're not quite ready yet? Well, once you start bringing romance back into your life or even if you're trying it out for the first time, you will start to experience a wonderful new mood inspired by your new love affair with your spouse. Start off slowly with the traditional romantic gestures like holding doors open, flowers, candy, little love letters and special attention to his or her needs. Once you make these romantic gestures habits in your marriage, you will find that your appetite for more romance and other similar moods will increase with time. You can satisfy your appetite with some fun and sensuous as well as romantic ideas.

Do you remember when you and your spouse were dating? It seemed as if you both couldn't get enough of each other. You most likely spent time holding hands, smiling at each other, whispering in one another's ears and all kinds of small little actions that kept your love exciting and new. Once a couple becomes married, they tend to stop doing those loving things after some time. Life becomes busy- you're walking too fast to get somewhere to hold hands, she knows you love her so you don't think you have to tell her, she might be offended if you order for her at a restaurant and so on. It is very easy to fall out of the habits of 'couples'. It can be just as easy to fall back in the habit if you give it a try.

Mort Katz once said that "Love is its own aphrodisiac and is the main ingredient for lasting sex." If you've got love and you're working on the romance, your own incredible love affair with your spouse is just waiting to break free! Do you know what turns your partner on? Are you aware of his or her most intimate, secret fantasies? Most people make assumptions about what their spouse likes based on external factors like what partners in previous relationships liked or what the latest magazine article claims to work. Everyone likes something different and in the bedroom is no exception. Now is the time to learn about your spouse, what you both want in the bedroom and what works for both of you as a couple.

One of the best parts about being married is being able to build an intimate relationship with someone special for the rest of your life. Intimacy is so very important to the success of every relationship. Romance can only take you so far. Many times it leads to intimacy but sometimes the intimacy still isn't triggered. Some couples require a little extra 'something' in order to get 'jump-started' in the bedroom. If you want to consider some creative ways to get creative in the bedroom or to simply spice up an existing love life, here are a few tips.

Whatever you choose to do, it will no doubt inspire more and more romantic ideas for your marriage. Once you have taken these ideas and your own have begun to blossom, cherish each one and make sure your spouse knows that every single idea is strictly for him or her!

This ends the first section. The next section will focus on small ideas that you can make use of to take your romance to another level.

CHAPTER SEVENTEEN

The Monster List

In this section of the book, we shall explore the various ways in which you can make your relationship and romance come alive. This chapter will focus on the aspect of creativity in romance and will provide a long, really long list of things that you can do in your relationship. Why is it that so many people believe that they don't have time or take the initiative to be romantic? Maybe most people don't believe that they are creative enough to be romantic. Everyone is creative! The definition of being creative is having the ability or power to create. The word create offers a much broader definition than most people accept when it comes to the process of being able to come up with something original or simply well thought out. Starting here, is a monster list of ideas that you could make use of.

1. When it comes to your relationship with your spouse and attempting to improve your marriage, you will most likely begin learning more and more about each other. This is a great way to get ideas for romantic planning as well as gifts for your spouse. Begin having conversations about your likes and dislikes with each other. Not only will taking about these things bring you closer together, but they can also help you express your love in an effective manner and buy gifts that he or she is sure to enjoy. If you want to do this in another, yet obvious way, you can make a specific checklist for both of you to complete. It is likely to cause all kinds of laughter and jokes at each other's expense, but this way you will have a concrete list on hand.

2. Start paying attention to what he or she likes. *Really* listen to what your spouse says, pay attention to the items he or she says he would like to try someday and get it for them. Don't give it to your spouse immediately and put the item away for a period of time. The period of time is up to you- it could be a week or it could be a month. When you think that he or she will no longer remember discussing the item with you, present it to them as a gift.

3. When you consider the number of likes and dislikes a person can have for just about everything in the world, it can seem a bit overwhelming. Start with simple things like his or her favorite color, lucky number(s), favorite music, favorite flower, favorite child's book, favorite current author, favorite singer, favorite song, favorite poet and favorite poem. You can then move on to their favorite food, favorite fruit, favorite vegetable, favorite type of chocolate, favorite cookie, favorite ice cream flavor, favorite snack food, favorite fast food and favorite restaurant.

4. Next, find out what your partner's favorite movie is (you might want to make this a 'top five' question- most people can't choose just one movie.) Then move on to find out who his or her favorite actress and actor are, their favorite romantic movie, comedy movie, musical, action movie and erotic movie. If you and or your spouse enjoy theater, now is the time to find out the specific of what they like about it. You can find out what their favorite play is, what their favorite show tune is and even who their favorite Broadway actor is.

5. Favorites can span all types of categories including sports and arts. Find out about their favorite artist, favorite style of artwork, favorite sculpture and favorite painting. Ask about his or her favorite sport to watch as well as their favorite sport to play. Take it further and find out about his or her favorite Olympic sport, favorite teams and even their favorite board game.

6. You can find out about more personal things like his or her favorite foreplay activity (both giving and receiving), their favorite position for making love, their favorite love making location, favorite sexy outfit (both his and hers), favorite place to be touched, favorite place to be kissed, favorite time of day to make love and their favorite fantasy. Find out their favorite place to shop for lingerie, their favorite color of lingerie and favorite style of lingerie.

7. Make note of what most might be considered to be small things like your spouse's favorite way to relax, his or her favorite television show, their favorite scent, favorite perfume or cologne, favorite beverage, favorite joke, favorite holiday, favorite day of the week and so much more. Take all of this information and treat it as the valuable resource that it is. Use it, update it and tweak it as often as necessary.

8. If you are searching for romantic ideas it is a good idea to keep a small notebook or voice recorder on your being so that you can make note of your ideas to use at a later date. Now is the time that you heighten your awareness

level as to what you hear and see with your spouse. Once you feel you have a good idea or feel for what he or she may enjoy, you can move on to other resources.

9. Take a look at your favorite magazine or newspaper. You will find that you most likely have a particular way you read the paper or skim through your magazine. Go back and look at everything you may have missed while skimming or flipping through the pages. Even one page with an incredibly romantic idea for you is worth the extra few minutes it takes to browse your reading material. Eventually, your eye will start skimming for this type of information automatically.

10. Pay attention to your spouse and what he or she pays attention to. If he is incredibly proud of his Italian heritage, it isn't exactly a hobby but an interest that can spark all kinds of romantic ideas for him. Some of the most common interests spouses notice with each other can include pets, comics, college, movies, books, golf, puzzles, food, shopping, clothes, music, specific wars throughout history and more. Can you think of something like these suggestions that you connect with your spouse? Would your spouse be able to say what your interests include? It could be an interesting exercise to have a discussion about with your spouse!

11. When you have 'received' all of the information you feel you need from and about your spouse, it's time to tweak your reception. You probably have an extensive list of information, but many items can most likely be fine-tuned even further. If his favorite color is green, do you know exactly what shade of green is his favorite? She loves chocolate, but does she love dark or milk chocolate more? Can you prepare your spouse's coffee for them to perfection?

12. Gifts that are considered to be traditionally romantic like candy and flowers are wonderful, but sometimes you need something that goes one step further. If your spouse enjoys flowers, you don't have to settle for roses because they can sometimes become unexciting after a while! Present him or her with something completely original such as a daisy or another flower where petals can be counted. Ask him or her to play the childhood game of 'they love me, they love me not' and watch them pluck the petals as they go. However, don't allow for the possibility of him or her arriving at the 'they love me not'. Count the petals before you present the flower to your spouse and trim it so that there are an odd number of petals for the right outcome!

13. Imagine stopping on the way home from work and picking wildflowers from alongside the road for your spouse. She may have had a

difficult day on the job, the kids were trying her patience or you both simply seem to have lost your intimacy lately. If you were to walk in the door with a fist full of wildflowers you took the time to select just for her on the way home; you will have broken the surrounding atmosphere with love and consideration. You both have the opportunity to start fresh with that one, small yet powerful gesture.

14. Arts and crafts used to be a fun break from the monotony of the school day, but believe it or not, it will come in handy when it comes to creative romantic gestures. Instead of promising that you will love him or her forever, show them. Take a piece of paper, ribbon or other material you choose and write "I love you" on both sides from end to end. Twist the paper 180 degrees and connect both ends of the paper until you have mad what looks like the figure eight. Tape or glue to ends together. You can present your love with a symbol that shows them your love for them is an endless love.

15. Creativity comes in many different forms! Being creative can mean creating an atmosphere. If you want to plan the ultimate romantic evening but funds are low or you simply don't want to have to leave the house, shut down the electricity and imitate a power outage (it's up to you whether or not you tell him or her!). You won't have any distractions or heat, so it is up to both of you to keep the other warm and entertain each other.

16. Maybe romance is on your mind, but he or she is going out of town. Did you know that people on airplanes are typically hopeless romantics? Any flight attendant would be more than happy to make sure that your spouse receives a special present after the flight has left the ground. Simply approach a crewmember after he or she boards the plane and they are usually more than happy to oblige a hopeless romantic like you! (You might want to make sure that the gift is unwrapped or keep it to a single rose due to heightened security.)

17. Creativity doesn't have to come in the form of gifts every single time. A gesture like getting up and dancing with your spouse when a special song comes up on the radio is quite creative and incredibly romantic! Whenever the mood strikes you, allow your creative juices to flow!

18. If you are going out of town or simply feel like 'ships passing in the night' because of kids, commitments or work, find a sun catcher, charm or porcelain figure in the shape of a star or a shooting star. Wrap the trinket in a small gift box and fold a note on top of it that says, "Wish you were here" and place it in his or her travel bag or even in a briefcase or purse. When he

or she finds it and knows that you are missing them and thought enough to share that sentiment, it will stir emotions that may not have been awakened in some time.

19. In order to change tedious or tired routines or to inspire intimacy, you might be surprised at how little effort is required. Tape a note on the television that says, "Wouldn't you rather turn me on?" instead. If he or she is enjoying a good book, remove the bookmark and replace it with a note that says, "I bet you'll never guess where I've hidden your bookmark."

20. Remember the small things you used to do when you first got together that would make your heart flutter and put a twinkle in your eye? Do them again! When you go shopping, for a walk or you're just sitting together watching TV, hold hands, link arms or put your arm around her. Softly whisper "Hey" into his or her ear and gaze lovingly into each other's eyes. If he or she wants to know what you are doing, simply say that you are amazed at how much you love them.

21. It is hard to find anyone who doesn't enjoy an Oreo cookie. Take an Oreo (or generic version of one), scratch the top of the cookie until smooth and then scratch a heart and your initials into the smooth surface. You can also make your own cookies and create personal messages. Another version is to make your own cupcakes and frost them with special messages in red icing. You can also give your spouse a true treat and track down a box of his or her favorite Girl Scout cookie.

22. Candy bars are always a special treat and you can use them as creative ways to send your spouse special messages. Hershey's Kisses are a favorite and many people already give them with their own special messages. You can also use other suggestive candy names like "Life Saver", "Mounds", "Fire Balls" and more. Instead of candy, you can fill the candy jar with love messages. On the other hand, you can fill the mailbox with candy.

23. Once you've satisfied your sweet tooth, take your spouse out to a large field, lie down and watch the clouds form different shapes. Not only are you out doing something fun together, but you are also far away from any distractions you might have at home. By the way if you didn't turn off your cell phone, you didn't have a truly romantic experience.

24. Did you know that over seventy five percent of women like stuffed animals and even more men enjoy electronic gadgets or power tools? These make perfectly fun gifts for both of you to be able to give to each other. An even better way to go about being a 'kid' with him or her is to find out what their favorite childhood item was and find it for them. It might mean a call

to his or her parents or a visit to EBay, but find it and let him or her know that every part of their life is important to you.

25. Comics are another wonderfully creative way to share your funny sense of humor and playful side with your spouse. Start combing the newspaper for funny comic strips and start to collect them. Tape them to the rearview mirror, the bathroom mirror, the refrigerator and even the back of the toilet seat. After you replace each comic strip, you can place the older ones in a scrapbook or photo album so that you enjoy them over and over again.

26. Guys, when you arrive at home with your wife, you can take this opportunity to 'sweep her off of her feet'- literally! Have you ever carried your wife over the threshold of your house? Well, it's a gesture that never gets old. The timing can be tricky with this one, though. Don't do it while either of you have a bag or bags in your hands or while she's on her cell phone. While the women may feel that this is an appropriate action to take with their men, it most likely won't work. If you feel you must give it a try, more power to you!

27. Create a home that is your romantic getaway location for both of you. Always keep a number of items that you can use in order to transform your home into a romantic hideaway. Keep a box filled with romantic scented candles, music, flowers and wine and keep some sensuous foods in the kitchen at all times. These can include strawberries, grapes, whipped cream and anything else that sparks your imagination.

28. When one spouse leaves a trail of clothes from the door all the way to the bedroom where they are waiting, it is always acceptable and a hit! You can also use a different version of this classic by leaving a trail of lit candles that lead to the bedroom. As always, the brightest burning flame should be that of the person waiting in the bedroom. Don't be surprised if your spouse's flame matches yours by the time he or she reaches the bedroom!

29. For romantic moments at the workplace, simply take the time at work to stop, call your spouse and tell them that you love them. Copy your face or a part of your body on the copy machine and send it to him or her with a funny or suggestive note. Send him or her flowers at the office or to the restaurant where he or she is having lunch. Mail him or her your contact information on a Rolodex card with a memo saying, "Love Source. Call when lonely or horny."

30. Make sure you check his or her schedule ahead of time before attempting this next move. Pack a pillow and a blanket in a picnic basket

and go to his or her office during the lunch hour. Tell his or her secretary to hold all calls, lock the office door and turn off every source of outside communication. Make love on the desk. It will most likely be some of the best sex you both have had in a long time and could become a habit!

31. Take a large, empty jar and use it so that each time you come up with what you think are spectacularly romantic ideas, you can write them down on small separate pieces of paper. Keep writing your ideas down until the jar is full. If your spouse wants to participate in this with you, he or she can add romantic ideas as well. About once each week, one of you must take an idea from the jar (no peeking) and they have to follow through on their selection within the following week.

32. Both spouses should be able to add to the jar at any time. If one spouse or both have a difficult time coming up with romantic ideas on their own, they can think about some of the most romantic movies that they've ever seen in order to try and come up with ideas. Another way to get ideas is to watch soap operas! While most of the story lines aren't something anyone wants to have to experience in their lifetime, some of the lines and gestures are incredibly romantic! You can also read a romance novel! They are chock full of what most women fantasize about with a man and you will have a unique perspective in being able to provide it to your spouse. If still come up empty, you check your local library or book store and take a look at the hundreds of books filled with all sorts of original romantic ideas.

33. Do you love a challenge? Create your own original search-a-word or crossword puzzle that contains important events in your lives or things that have special meaning to both of you. You can include things like where you went on your honeymoon, where he or she proposed, private jokes, pet names, favorite songs, favorite time of day or anything else that makes you think of your spouse.

34. When you feel that your creativity just won't cut it and you want to present your spouse with a gift, it might not be an opportune time to get in the car, go to the store and take the time to pick up something special. Instead of always waiting until you are approaching a special occasion or you simply need something 'last minute', why not start picking up little gifts here and there for your spouse and put them away in a secret hiding place to be used later on? You can also save money by shopping for your spouse this way when you buy items on sale or discounted, when you buy in bulk or simply when you see something you are sure your spouse would love. You will always be prepared for any type of special occasion or no particular

occasion at all!

35. While being romantic often draws to mind gifts and planning outings together, you don't have to spend money in order to be romantic! You can plan a day where you are completely at your spouse's disposal. Devote yourself entirely to your spouse for an entire day. He or she can ask you to do chores, rub their feet, give them a massage, watch a movie you normally wouldn't watch together or try an interest of his or hers that you haven't tried. Your spouse may also decide that you are best put to use in the bedroom!

36. When you want to do something extra special, take your spouse on a local 'honeymoon' trip! Find a local hotel that has a honeymoon suite and book it for one night. Do it up right and make sure it is stocked with champagne, strawberries and whipped cream. Have flowers and your song available to play in your room. For her, have new lingerie laid out on the bed. For him, have new lingerie laid out on the bed. For an extra special twist, pack a bag for your spouse, hire a sitter if necessary and tell him or her that you're going out for the evening. Blindfold your spouse and lead him or her to your honeymoon suite.

37. Find an affordable card shop or see if your local greeting card store offers any type of multiple card purchase discounts. Buy as many cards for your spouse as you can. Store the cards and send them to your spouse intermittently. You can choose to send them every few months, every month, every week, each day or every waking hour!

38. Take the time to create your own loving edible baked goods for your spouse! Make heart shaped cookies, a heart shaped cake or make your own heart shaped chocolates. Find a heart shaped bowl, pop popcorn to serve in the bowl and spend the entire day watching romantic movies together.

39. Keep shopping all of the time. This doesn't mean that you should just load up your shopping basket each time you head out. This doesn't require much effort and you will most likely go broke doing this! Instead, each time you are in a store with or without your spouse, keep an eye out for items you think he or she would love to have or find touching. Pay attention when you are together either window shopping or looking for specific items. If he or she finds something that they have an interest in, either purchase it when they aren't close by or come back later and buy it for them.

40. You can find all kinds of wonderful treasures in a variety of shops. Try browsing shops you don't enter on a regular basis for ideas and many times, rare finds. Some of these types of shops include antique stores, new

and used bookstores, second-hand shops, toy stores, video stores, sporting goods stores, nostalgia shops, natural health food stores, card shops and more.

41. When you go shopping, head out without any preconceived ideas. Use your intuition to shop for your partner. In other words, don't find your gift- let your gift find you! If your spouse has a favorite store that he or she loves, get to know the manager and other employees. Stop in on a regular basis to see if he or she has been in and shown any interest in a particular item. Buy it!

42. Always be ready to buy something while you are out. Keep a 'gift buying' fund tucked safely in the back of your wallet so that you are never without funds. Try to pay cash, as your partner shouldn't be able to find out what you spend through credit card receipts or statements. Because you will most likely be accumulating gifts faster than you are giving them, make sure you have a safe hiding spot in which you can store your gifts.

43. Jewelry is an incredibly popular gift for one spouse to present to another. Jewelry is often exchanged on holidays like Christmas, Anniversaries, Valentine's Day and other days celebrating special events. Did you know that jewelry is the most appreciated when it is given without any particular requirement like a holiday or specific celebration? If you are considering a romantic gesture, you should think about presenting your spouse with jewelry for no particular reason at all.

44. Diamonds are always a popular choice when it comes to jewelry, but gold, silver and other gemstones on their own can be just as popular. Did you that each month has a gemstone dedicated to it and each gemstone has its own special symbolic meaning? If you really want to blow him or her away, you can select a particular gemstone because of it's the significance it has with a particular month or because of its own special meaning. There are twelve months in the year, so there are twelve gemstones with their own significant meaning. January's gemstone is a garnet and it represents faith and stability. February's gemstone is amethyst and it represents sincerity and happiness. March's gemstone is aquamarine and represents hope and bravery. April's gemstone is a diamond, which represents joy and innocence. May's gemstone is an emerald and represents peace and tranquility. June's gemstone is a pearl, which represents wisdom and pureness. July's gemstone is a ruby and it represents passion and nobility. August's gemstone is sardonyx and it stands for power and joy. September's gemstone is a sapphire, which represents honesty and hope. October's

gemstone is an opal and stands for confidence and sweet love. November's gemstone is topaz and it stands for friendship and faithfulness. December's gemstone is turquoise, which stands for understanding and success.

45. Sometimes the delivery of the jewelry is almost as important as the selection of the right piece. There are movies and personal accounts of how individuals have delivered a special trinket to their loved ones. One of the most popular delivery methods seems to be through food! People either place a ring or other piece of jewelry in champagne or other clear beverage or they bake the jewelry into a special treat like a pie or cake. What you don't hear about in these stories is that you have to be careful of a few things. First of all, make sure your loved one doesn't choke on their gift! Secondly, check with your jeweler before placing any type of jewelry in food. Did you know that rubies crack when they are heated and that pearls will dissolve in champagne?

46. On your next birthday, celebrate your spouse and how he or she makes your existence better by presenting him or her with a gift. He or she will be so surprised that you might see a tear or two of joy fall.

47. Take over a chore or daily task for your spouse without letting them know about your intentions. Mow the lawn, washing the car, cook and clean up from meals or clean the house- do something substantial for him or her. If you find that he or she loved having the break from a particular task, do it over and over again as often as you can.

48. One of the most recognizable symbols of a celebration is a balloon! Fill your car with balloons and take them home to him or her. Fill the living room before he or she gets home from work. Make sure you have some balloons marked with your names in hearts on them and some should have personal messages written as well. Begin the celebration of your love today.

49. Start celebrating each major and minor holiday with your spouse. Begin with New Year's Eve and do it big. Go to New York City and go to Times Square if that's as big as you can think! Valentine's Day should be done as lavishly as possible. On the Fourth of July, plan to attend the most extravagant fireworks display you can find or plan on making fireworks of your own at home. Always celebrate each other's birthdays and do it with flair. Your Anniversary should be a special day and celebrated with an expensive bottle of your favorite drink. Get dressed up on Halloween as your favorite fantasy characters and role-play for the entire evening. Celebrate any and every day you want by staying home from work and playing in bed. Celebrate as often of infrequently as you want to, but make

sure you take the time to play, surprise each other and celebrate your relationship.

50. One of the most romantic nights of the year couples spend together is New Year's Eve. Couples love to get dressed up in their best, often new clothes to head out for a celebration with friends and/or family. Instead of going out for New Year's Eve this year, tell your spouse that you want to celebrate the beginning of another year together alone at home. Stay home, be comfortable, buy champagne, light the fire, turn on some soft music and snuggle up with your spouse the entire evening. It will be one of the most memorable New Year's Eves you'll have and don't be surprised if it becomes your new yearly tradition!

51. Another holiday dedicated to love and romance is definitely Valentine's Day. While most spouses go with the traditional chocolates and roses, you aren't going to this year. Be creative and think about what he or she truly loves. If it's flowers, buy an assortment of flowers that begin with the first letter of his or her name. If he or she loves books, choose authors according to a similarly personal theme.

52. Aside from special occasions throughout the year, you have the opportunity to be romantic each and every day. For example, if you are lucky enough to be able to sit down for any meal of the day together don't turn on the television or pick up the newspaper to read. Ask him or her how their day was, what they are planning to do or make plans to spend the upcoming weekend together. You can also use this discussion time to listen to your partner and begin offering compromises instead of simply arguing. You will find that he or she will be much more responsive and likely to give in a little to what you want as well!

53. Making love together can be a wonderfully fulfilling experience. It can be even more so when you add romantic gestures to your love making. Most couples decide to make love right before going to sleep at night. Instead of 'just doing it', take the time to offer your partner more stimulation for foreplay. He or she will not refuse! Try new things and listen to your partner for feedback. His or her responses may not be in words, but you will be able to tell what is working and what's not working. Take your time. Both of you will enjoy the rewards by slow, considerate and thorough lovemaking.

54. For the husbands that have no idea where to begin with their wives, you can always start with a day at the mall. Prepare a shopping list of specific items or stores you know she either frequents or would enjoy

receiving a gift from. If you still feel quite clueless as to what you buy your wife, here is your own shopping list guaranteed to thrill her. Begin at a bath shop and buy her lotion, bath gel and/or powder.

55. Next, visit a lingerie shop. If you are unsure of your wife's size, ask the employees for help. There is no need to be embarrassed and they are more than happy to assist you in your search.

56. Locate a fine and reputable jewelry store. If you are unsure of your wife's ring size, stick to a necklace, bracelet or brooch.

57. Stop by a liquor store and pick up her favorite bottle of wine or a bottle of champagne for no particular reason other than to celebrate each other.

58. Your next stop should be the flower shop where you can pick out her favorite flowers or a simple rose.

59. Finally, you will need a card to accompany all of your purchases. If you prefer, you can make your own card or write a personalized love letter instead. Make sure that all of her gifts are wrapped separately and enjoy the pleasure you both will get from your efforts!

60. Now for the wives who want to do something extra special and romantic for their husbands. You can either buy him a romantic card or write him a personal love letter before sealing the envelope and sealing it with a kiss. Make sure you use the reddest lipstick you have for the kiss and then mail it to him. For a variation on this idea, spray a card or note with your perfume.

61. Try and do your best not to become a choice between him and his passions, whether they are sports, computers, etc. He was once a huge fan of yours and you simply have to remind him of that at make it worth his while to be your fan once again. If you have trouble understanding your man in your relationship, take the time to discover what it is about him that makes him who he is. Robert Bly and Rachel Snyder have some wonderfully entertaining and insightful books to assist you on this subject. Not only will you be able to understand your husband a little better, but you will be able to increase your intimacy level and trust as a result of your efforts.

62. Look at your spouse. Really *look* at him or her. Make mental notes about all of the things you find attractive and admire about your mate. If something crosses your mind that could be considered negative, immediately erase it from your mind. It doesn't matter when you teach yourself to focus on the good qualities. Start to compliment him or her several times a day. Pace yourself and commit to giving him or her a

compliment at regular intervals like every four to six hours. If you have a watch with a timer on it you can use that until you get in the habit of doing it on your own, which will happen naturally.

63. Just as you take the time to have at least three meals a day, make sure you tell your spouse that you love them at least three times a day. Successfully romantic couples know that the first thing they should say to each other in the morning before anything else is "I love you" and they mean it. They look into their partner's eyes and make sure they say that they love the other person with feeling. Begin your day by telling you partner you love them and continue at your own discretion. Another great action to accompany your expression of love or to be used all on its own is to give your spouse a hug. Hug tightly, hug gently, hug for a long time, hug quickly, but be sure to hug often.

64. When you have a problem with your body, you often go to see a doctor to have it fixed or cured. Treat romance in your relationship the same way a doctor would treat a patient, except you are the doctor and your spouse is the patient. While you are always welcome to play 'doctor' in the bedroom, these are ideas that lead to creating romance both in and out of the bedroom. Have you heard that the green M&M's can help arouse a person? While there is no scientific research to support such a claim, it is a fun and interesting idea! Take an empty aspirin bottle and fill it only with green M&M's. Label it appropriately including your spouse's name, what the medication is, any side effects, dosage, how many refills are available and the doctor's name that prescribed the medication. Place it on his or her bedside table or along with the other medications or daily vitamins they take.

65. Another version of this idea is to take a bottle of a great smelling lotion or oil and label it is if it should be used like a prescription. You might want to select fragrances like vanilla or musk that are said to have an aphrodisiac effect!

66. You most likely have life insurance for both you and your spouse, so why don't you have a warranty for you and your spouse? Show your love and commitment by presenting your wife or husband with a lifetime relationship warranty. Be as specific as possible on your warranty! List your commitment and devotion on several pages if you must, but make sure you 'guarantee' your dedication to the growth of your relationship.

67. Selfless acts are exceptional ways to show your love and they can be very romantic. Imagine you are both up early getting ready for work and it

is ice cold outside. You go about your routine, but you try to make it outside a good five to ten minutes before he or she does. You start their car, turn the heat all the way up and brush off the snow (if any) so that when they come out to head off to their destination they have you to thank for your thoughtful foresight and initiative. A warm car on an icy morning is one of the most creatively romantic gestures you can offer your spouse.

68. Mark your calendar each week to remind yourself to take the time a write down something wonderful about your spouse. It could a reason why you love him or her, one thing he or she did that you thought was wonderful, an inspirational thought inspired by him or her or all of these ideas. At the completion of a year, print out all of your thoughts on a long piece of paper and present it to him or her as a scroll wrapped with a ribbon.

69. Unless your job requires constant communication with work because you are a doctor, firefighter, etc., you need to stop depending on your multimedia and electronic devices for a good amount of time each week. You can do this however suits both you and your spouse best, whether it be random days, an entire weekend or any other time that works for you. Disconnect from your cell phone, computer (this includes email) television, radio and even the newspaper or magazines. You and your spouse need to spend time together without the distractions all forms of media present on a daily basis. You will find yourself looking forward to this time once you get used to not having to jump each time you hear your cell phone or worrying about what you missed in your email. You will learn that it call all wait and is far less important that the time you are spending with your spouse.

70. You know the big cardboard box that the new appliance was delivered in? You remember because it caused some financial strain between you and your spouse. It was also a source of conflict because you both had something different in mind when picking it out. Take the big cardboard box and make a card out of it. Simply cut out two of the larger sides keeping the natural fold as the center of your card, tape or glue paper bags to cover up and unwanted wording on the outside and make the biggest card he or she will ever receive. The sentiment is up to you, as you know best what he or she needs to hear.

71. Make a jumbo sized banner for your love. Tape construction paper together or you can order a banner just by doing a quick search on the Internet. Try to make your banner at least 12 feet long and decorate it yourself. You can get stencils at your local craft store if your handwriting simply won't compliment your effort.

72. Have you ever seen your local high school(s) holding fundraisers? You can offer your local high school's marching band, choir or other entertainment ensemble a donation in order to serenade your spouse at home. Imagine the surprise on your spouse's face when he or she hears their favorite song playing live from the front yard! If you go for something this big, make sure you remember to videotape it so that you can relive it over and over again.

73. As you and your partner begin exploring your romantic sides and you are both providing new and creative ways in which to express your love for one another, you may find that you want to do what you can to hold on to as many of these memories as possible. Consider starting a 'memory' chest or box with your spouse where you can place all of the important and considerate items that will remind you how romantic your experiences have been.

74. If you and your spouse have started to enjoy spending nights out on the town together, you can begin by saving what you collect while you are out and about. Keep all of your theater ticket stubs, movie theater stubs, concert ticket stubs and even restaurant receipts if you choose. If you eat somewhere that offers matchbooks or something comparable, you might want to begin picking one up and putting it in a special box when you arrive at home. For a more organized version of this, those who love scrapbooking can create a scrapbook around these items or you can simply place them in photo albums so that you and your spouse can go back to see all that you have experienced together.

75. Some couples love to go on vacation together and romance can play a huge role in most of them. Tropical or mild vacation destinations are quite popular and can provide a number of romantic items that can return home at little or no cost. You can collect shells or fill a small bottle of sand marked with the beach it came from to keep at home. I know one family that collected seashells and surrounded the base of their swimming pool with them! For couples that prefer to take both tropical and wintry vacations, the colder climates provide similarly beautiful trinkets for couples to collect like pinecones and even melted snow!

76. If you and your spouse enjoy wine and/or champagne, start saving the labels and corks from the bottles. You can save them in plastic bags marked with the occasion and any other notable information from when the beverage was used. For couples who enjoy road trips, keep maps from all of the journeys you've taken together or keep a large map on the wall at home

so that you can mark where you've been with pushpins.

77. Make your own special memories just by staying at home. Challenge each other romantically by trying to agree on the most romantic kiss that has even been in a movie. Buy that movie and try to recreate that kiss with each other! Place the movie in your memory box and revisit it frequently. If you can't agree on just one kiss, name the top five and repeat the aforementioned steps with all five! Next, try and agree on the most romantic song ever made. Buy the CD (or download the single and burn it) and dance with each other to that song. Place the song in your memory box and again, dance to it frequently.

78. Does your spouse like things a little over the top? Maybe he or she loves things that are truly outrageous. Or maybe it's you that loves the outrageous situation or event. Romance can be suited to your 'over the top' or 'extreme' tastes. Be outrageous and do something completely unexpected in order to surprise and romance your spouse. If you're looking to overdo something slightly, do something traditional in a big way. When you think of or come across a romantic idea, magnify it with your imagination and do it as big as you think.

79. Singing to your partner is one of the most romantic things that you can do. Why not take your spouse to a karaoke bar and surprise (maybe even shock!) him or her by singing a song that has special meaning for both of you. Enjoy him or her watching you with laughter and possibly tears in their eyes. It is outrageous enough to never forget, unless you both hit the bars every week.

80. Think about something your spouse loves. I mean that they really, really love. If he or she loves Hershey Kisses, find the biggest glass jar you can and fill it with his or her favorite kind. Mix and match flavors for a twist! If you feel that the largest jar isn't enough, remove all of his or her clothes from a dresser drawer and fill the empty drawer to the brim with his or her favorite treat. Leave a little note on top expressing your love for your spouse.

81. Commit to making love as often as possible with your spouse for an extended period of time. Change your attitude about how you view sex at the end of a long, tiring day. Try looking forward to it and make sure you make love every day and/or night for at least a week. Try to go for a month. Among most married couples today, this is truly outrageous!

82. Set the timer on your watch or cell phone so that it goes off each and every hour. If you know that he or she is on the computer all day,

send emails reminding them that you love them. Send a message on the cell phone or call your spouse just to say that you love them.

83. Hire a service that specializes in skywriting. Have them write a special message to your spouse in the sky! You'll be outside when he or she sees your message. Take a walk to the nearest pool, pond or lake and go skinny-dipping! Be outrageously in love with each other!

84. Post-it notes can be addictive once you start using them. Use them to go overboard by leaving post-it love notes everywhere! You don't have to make them all about love. You can make them silly notes, romantic poems quotes, song lyrics, riddles, sexy and teasing notes or any other topic that works for you and your spouse. You can post them all at once all over or you can pace yourself daily, weekly or monthly.

85. When was the last time you played with your spouse? I mean *really* played with him or her with laughter and teasing. Life and love does not have to be serious all of the time. If it is, you will have a dull life and a joyless marriage. You may not think about yourself as playful, but it's time that you did. Play with your wife. Play with your husband. Make jokes about yourself and each other (silly jokes, not hurtful ones). Play water tag with the sprayer at the kitchen sink. Take a piece of masking tape and write a silly word like "dork" on it. Sneak up behind your spouse, slap the tape on his or her arm and say, "Tag! You're it!" There's nothing wrong with having some childish fun with your spouse. The best part might just be the look on your spouse's face when you unexpectedly make the first move!

86. Start playing games with each other on a regular basis. You can play board games or you can make up games of your own. Try role-playing games! They can be plain silly or they can turn into very intimate encounters. The wonderful thing about playing games with your spouse is that you learn a great deal about each other while building trust. You can even reenact wonderful times you've had together. If you had an incredible first date, go back to the place you had your date, relive the moments and even try to reenact the most special moments.

87. You may not know about it, but you might actually know a couple whom already plays a very common yet private game among couples. It's basically a 'hide and seek' game that goes on, well, forever! You and your spouse choose an object and you each take turns to 'return' it to the other in creative ways. Some spouses have had the objects expressed mailed to them, others hid it in a place special to their spouse and other couples used intermediate individuals to deliver the object like flight attendants or

waiters.

88. True trust can come from playing games in the bedroom- as well as a ton of fun! Start your morning by planning to make love that night. Try to keep 'foreplay' going all day long. Call your spouse with reminders and teasers about what is going to happen, what you want to do and how your partner makes you feel. By the time you both reach the bedroom, you will both feel as if you've spent hours at foreplay.

89. Play some fun games while you're out with your spouse. When you are at the mall, commit to kissing every time you see another couple holding hands. (Unfortunately, you might not be kissing as often as you think.) Kiss at each stop sign or stop light. Make love at unusual locations like changing rooms, rest stops or restrooms.

90. Role-playing is a popular game among adults. One of the most popular role-playing games is to pretend you aren't married and you are having an affair with each other. Carry out all of the actions you think might be involved in an affair including how you would act, what you would do and where you would go.

91. Make your romantic life with your spouse a weekly game. Do you remember the old board game spinning wheels? If you can find one, remove the spinner from a board game you no longer use. Cover the original instructions on the wheel with paper and separate it equally into twelve sections. Fill in the sections with a romantic activity and you and your spouse can take turns spinning the wheel each day or once a week.

92. Most communities hold a variety of carnivals and festivals throughout the year. Even those who live in climates that change drastically from warm summers to cold and snowy winters continue to have summer, harvest, winter and spring festivals. Take your spouse to any or all of them! Make sure you eat some of the food there, play some games, try and win a prize, ride the rides if there are any and buy your love a trinket to remember the day by.

93. Take a day to spend at the mall, but you won't be spending the entire day with each other. You and your spouse each get a specific amount of money (about ten dollars- no more than twenty) to spend while you're there. You both agree to shop for a certain amount of time and return to the same place you started. Here's where it becomes romantic- you are only allowed to buy trinkets for each other while you shop. Some couples make up their own shopping theme and they can only buy items that fit that theme. For example, if you are close to a holiday like Christmas, only shop

for Christmas related items. Maybe you both need a good laugh and you can only shop for gag gifts. Use your creative side to make a day out 'together' fun!

94. If you really want to have fun, you can enjoy dressing up for each other. Not the way you dress up to go out to dinner, but the way you used to dress up to go out on Halloween! Visit a local costume shop and rent what you both have chose for the other. Make a night of it- at home!

95. Think about and know exactly when all of your special anniversaries are with your spouse. You should, of course, know your wedding day, but what about the first day you met each other? You should know and celebrate the first time you kissed, the first time you made love, your first major fight, your first date, your first home together, the first time one of you said, "I love you", and even the day you believed you conceived your first child (and each consecutive child). Blow your spouse away when you begin to celebrate these special occasions in the life you share together.

96. If you think you've surprised your spouse by your sudden interest in celebrating your special moments together, you'll no doubt have the urge to surprise your spouse over and over again in different ways. There are many different types of surprises you can plan in order to impress your spouse. There are surprise you can pull off only once in a lifetime, surprises that are so unexpected that they can only be called a total surprise, shocking surprises, surprises at work, funny surprises, big surprises and little surprises. There are expensive as well as inexpensive surprises, out-of-character surprises, private surprises, public surprises, group surprises and meaningful surprises.

97. In order to pull of great surprises, you really need to know your spouse and how he or she will react to certain situations. If he or she tends to be quite shy, private and shies away from being the center of attention, you might not want to plan a group surprise like a birthday party or propose to her all over again in the middle of a restaurant. Quiet or private dinners or walks on the beach are better places for these types of surprises. If you want to surprise your spouse at work, make sure that it is acceptable for whatever you plan to happen at his or her particular workplace. You don't want the surprise to be his or her being reprimanded for an unacceptable event.

98. One of the most popular and well-received types of surprises is a sexy surprise. Sexy surprises often happen in the bedroom, but they can happen elsewhere as well. For example, if he takes you out to dinner you can wear very sexy lingerie underneath your clothes. Halfway through dinner,

excuse yourself to go to the ladies' room and unbutton your blouse enough for him just be able to see that you are wearing something he'll obviously want to see more of. Guys can buy a special pair of undergarments and pass her a note halfway through dinner asking her to guess what's different about him- in his pants! Use your creativity and make sure that both of you are comfortable no matter what surprise you have in store.

99. Start to think about everything you do as an activity or opportunity for the both of you. If you have to go out of town on a business trip, take your spouse with you. While you're away or even while you're at home together, take turns reading the newspaper aloud in bed. Make sure you read the funnies to each other and you must use appropriate voices for different characters!

100. Take entire days together to go out and explore new things. Buy a book that lists all of the attractions in yours and surrounding areas. Visit each place that neither one of you has been to before. Go on treasure hunts to places like flea markets, auctions, antique shops, second-hand stores, garage sales, craft sales and church rummage sales. These are great places to pick up gifts for your spouse that you save for a later date.

101. While most people know about 'his and hers' items like bathrobes and towels, there are a number of other items that can be enjoyed together as 'couples' items. Try getting matching motorcycles along with matching T-shirts. Have matching his and hers overnight bags, coffee mugs, bicycles, cell phones, cars, holiday ornaments, tennis rackets, rocking chairs and even matching carved pumpkins on Halloween.

102. Go shopping together and work on finding something for him and something for her. Go to a bookstore and select a book that you know your spouse will like and have him or her do the same for you. Go to a music store and select a CD you know that your spouse will like and again, have him or her do the same for you. Find other ways to apply this same concept to other specialty stores.

103. At the beginning of each month, sit down together as a couple and review your calendars. Make all of your plans that you will do together before working in all of your other appointments and commitments into your schedule. Your relationship commitments should always come first and be your top priority. Couples who keep their relationship first in their lives have the most enviable relationships.

104. Start your week off on Sunday and keep in mind that it is a wonderful day to remain low-key and enjoy time alone with your spouse.

Take a long walk without cell phones, iPods or any other distracting devices. Just you and your spouse should take a walk and enjoy each other's company. Hold hands while you walk. You can also spend the day in your bedroom, keep the curtains drawn and light some candles. You are in charge of whatever else happens there. On the other hand, you can spend the entire day in bed with the curtains open and read the paper to each other or watch movies all day. Eat your meals in bed. (Making love is definitely an option as well!) Sundays are typically a 'day of rest' for many, but that doesn't mean that you must lounge around the house or park your being in front of the television all day! Most towns and larger cities publish their own guidebook that lists all types of attractions for locals and tourists to visit. Your city might even have a web site with this type of information. Find something you and your spouse have never done or visited before and go together.

105. On Monday, wake up with the birds. Enjoy a morning together without the normal rush you typically go through. Go to a music store and buy a romantic CD to present to your spouse. Enjoy it together before going to bed. Mondays are also great for calling in sick to repeat an exceptional Sunday again. On Monday, celebrate the birth of your spouse! It doesn't have to be his or her birthday in order to celebrate the fact that they were born. Find a book or greeting card that lists all of the special events that have happened on the day that they were born throughout history or find a list of famous people who share his or her birthday. Also, you can find their horoscope for the year, week or day and present it to them as a birthday wish.

106. Tuesdays are great days to wake up early and begin making love with your spouse. On another Tuesday, try reading something you both find to be inspirational aloud. As an alternative activity for particularly busy Tuesdays, send your spouse loving thoughts by using telepathy. You don't think it works? Try it and you'll see. On Tuesday, make it an extra special good-bye when you leave each other for work or other commitment. Kiss for a long time or enjoy a nice long embrace. Continue to look back at him or her while you walk toward your car or the door.

107. Wednesdays are always difficult days of the week because they are only the halfway mark to the anticipated weekend. Do something different like taking a class together, give each other massages (or just give him or her a massage) or have dinner together. In fact, pack a picnic lunch, meet him or her at work and either eat there or leave to eat at a park or even in the car. On Wednesday, play the lottery or buy some of the instant win tickets

that you must scratch in order to win money. Let him or her know that you don't need any because you won the lottery when you met them.

108. You must remember that Thursday is always gift day. When you are at a store and you spot something your spouse might enjoy or you know he or she will love, you should start picking those items up and storing them for Thursdays. You should never run out of gifts this way and you must never miss gift day! On Thursday (and all subsequent Thursdays), you need to present your spouse with a gift. Simply mark Thursday on your calendar as gift day.

109. On Friday, take the time to reminisce about all that you have done together, whether it is looking through a photo album, watching home movies or simply sitting together and talking about great memories. Be careful not to touch on subjects that could lead to resurrecting hurt feelings or bad memories (it's okay to have them- just don't re-visit them during your 'romance' time). Avoid anything that will remind you of arguments or of family members that cause friction between you and your spouse. Friday is always a day to look forward to! When your spouse comes home from work, have 'your' song playing on the radio. If you took dance classes together on Wednesday, they will come in handy! Draw him or her a bath and share it together.

110. Saturday is your day to be creative. Think about his or her favorite artist (music, painting, sculpture, etc.) and buy them some of their work. Make love, but make up some fun rules like you can't open your eyes or you can't use your hands. Make a decadent dessert and feed it to each other. Saturday's romance mission will be of cuddling, touching and enjoying each other more. Start all over again when you wake up Sunday morning!

111. Most new relationships or new beginnings rely on the 'little' things to show love and affection. Be sure to remember special 'couple' days like Valentine's Day, Anniversaries and even the date you met if possible. Be sure to send a meaningful gift or just a dozen roses and a box of chocolates to celebrate your feelings for your partner. Women can do exactly the same thing for men here. Not many men can resist candy!

112. You may not consider yourself to be a writer, but writing your partner a long love letter with your thoughts about how you feel for the other person is one of the most touching ways to spark romance. If you aren't comfortable writing a letter, consider making lists about what you love the most about your partner. Lists can be about the things they do that makes you laugh, what they do for you that you appreciate, how they make

you feel inside, how beautiful or handsome they are and other very personal but attentive details.

113. Call your partner and talk softly and lovingly. If he or she isn't able to answer the phone, leave loving messages on their voice mail or answering machine. Talk dirty when you know that he or she can't return the same conversation on the other end.

114. Sometimes couples feel more comfortable trying to bring romance into their relationship by bestowing gifts on their partner. While classics like flowers, candy and perfume or cologne are almost always successful gifts, try 'giving' something different. Make plans to go see every romantic movie that comes to the theater during the year. Bring home a bottle of champagne to celebrate even the tiniest accomplishment he or she has had. Randomly send romantic and/or humorous greeting cards to his or her workplace or hide them under the bed pillows at home.

115. When you find that you are ready to implement romantic acts into your daily routine with your spouse, be creative with what you can come up with. For example, you can buy decorative pillows for the bedroom with "Tonight" and "Not Tonight" printed on either side. You can use this as your own private signal for each other and your intentions. Other couples will use more subtle indications as to their intentions with you in the bedroom.

116. When you want to think of your own, you can make up your own 'code' to say whenever the mood strikes you. Maybe your wife will say "I'm getting tired" and then you can say, "Well, then let's get you to bed." Try something even more subtle like saying the same word three times in the same sentence like 'blue' or another obvious word. Walk up to your partner and begin humming 'your song' in his or her ear. Pull a Carol Burnett and tug on your ear lobe- whatever you both agree on will be a small form of your own private foreplay that will make you want to rush home and make love!

117. Sometimes it takes something extra special that both you and your partner enjoy to get in the mood like chocolate! Chocolate is one of the few things that most men and women share a love for and never tire of. You can use chocolate in a number of ways to spark romance or initiate a little foreplay with your partner. You can always, of course, present your spouse with a gift of their favorite chocolate and that is sometimes enough to get him or her in the mood. Try bringing his or her favorite chocolates to bed one night and feed each other. You can always be selfish and only allow your spouse to lick off what melts on your fingers. Also, you can 'accidentally'

get some melted chocolate on your spouse! Lick it off, say that it tastes so much better on them and do it again and again!

118. Make plans to take a vacation completely focused on chocolate together! Two of the world's most famous chocolate factories are the Nestle chocolate factory in Broc, Switzerland and the Hershey Chocolate factory in Hershey, Pennsylvania. Some people even believe that chocolate is an aphrodisiac. Why not test this theory on your own chocolate vacation fantasy?

119. When you go anywhere together, start putting your arm in his or take her arm and enter that way- enter as a couple. Even before that, make sure you never walk without holding his or her hand. Take a look at elderly couples that have obviously been married a long time. They still hold hands.

120. After living together for some time, it is most likely that you have accumulated some of the same types of clothing. Intentionally match your outfits now and then! If you don't want to go that far, buy matching coats or caps and wear those when you are out together. It doesn't have to be every time you leave the house, but every once in a while should be fun!

121. When you take your wife out, it's still okay to do the traditional things men used to do for women. Although feminism is very real and should be taken seriously, there is nothing wrong with holding the door open for your wife or pulling her chair out for her to sit at the table. These are not signs of a weak woman who cannot do it herself. You are showing her respect each time that you make a gesture like that.

122. Flirt subtly with each other whenever you feel like it! You don't have to be out to dinner or at a party to flirt with each other. Do it at home while you're cleaning the kitchen or while he or she's reading a book. Walk by and whisper their pet name in their ear or plant a kiss on his or her neck. Make eye contact and wink or offer a seductive smile. Take the initiative and do what comes naturally.

123. For those who are uncomfortable with public displays of affection or even private displays of affection, give it a try. If you find that you are unable to enjoy little attempts at being affectionate, you might want to seek counseling to discover why it makes you feel that way. If you and your spouse are happy without that type of affection, more power to you but it is unlikely that *both* of you are content. It doesn't hurt to try and the worst that can happen is that you might actually like it!

124. Visit some of the most popular lingerie stores in your area together or browse web sites like Victoria's Secret or Frederick's of Hollywood. You

can even request catalogs to be delivered to your home so that you can 'shop' together at your leisure. Have him mark off what he finds exciting and arousing. Have her mark off what she finds exciting and arousing. Both should go through the catalog or shop together and make note of what they both agree on. Then both spouses should put all of their preconceived ideas and judgments aside as they explore possibilities with and for each other. To begin with, wives should try something incredibly simple yet incredibly sexy like laying on a bed of black sheets while wearing white lingerie or the other way around. That is a wonderful starting point and safe way to open up about what you both enjoy in the bedroom.

125. Look into what is considered to be an aphrodisiac and try some things out together. An aphrodisiac is anything like a smell, drug, food, drink or even flower that some say increase or stimulates sexual desire. While scientific evidence to back the actual effectiveness of aphrodisiacs is lacking, some couples find excitement simply in trying new things. Some of the most common things people claim to have an aphrodisiac affect include hot, sweat producing spices, oysters, wasabi, caviar reinforced by vodka, ginseng, yohimbe and the scents of musk, patchouli and vanilla. Two flowers that are thought to be related to sex enhancement are the Hibiscus and Calla Lilies.

126. If you and your spouse have a difficult time sitting down and telling each other about your sexual fantasies, try making a game out of it. Get a large, empty jar and fill it with 25 of your most intimate sexual fantasies. You can make them anything that has to with your fulfilment, your spouse's fulfilment or both of your fulfilment. Again, setting all inhibitions and judgments aside, you both get to pick a single fantasy each week that should be fulfilled as a couple. It is up to both of you if you feel the need to set particular rules and/or boundaries. Of course, the game can always change as you both grow more comfortable with each other and learn how much fun and fulfilling being intimate with your own spouse can be.

127. Being 'naughty' is quite a turn-on for most men and women in the bedroom. What one person might consider being naughty might feel or seem completely normal to another person. In order to enjoy intimate growth, it is important to be comfortable with your own sexuality. This is something that you can work on on your own, with your spouse or with the help of a qualified professional.

128. Fill the back of your car with 'comfort' items like pillows and blankets. Take him or her for a drive in the country. You've got the tools

and the imagination to take it from there. If you are looking to make it truly interesting, wear something truly risqué and slowly undress revealing bits of you lingerie at a time to your spouse while you head out to the country (make sure the driving is safe, though!). The men can do the same!

129. One thing that most men tend to enjoy in the bedroom but never really talk about is when he and/or his spouse engage in 'talking dirty'. Talking dirty can mean a lot of things to a lot of different people, so they type of dirty talk can vary from relationship to relationship. First of all, talk to your spouse if you have an interest in trying to talk dirty while making love. If you feel comfortable enough with your spouse, simply try a little bit and watch for his or her reactions the next time you make love. Some women in particular feel that they wouldn't even know where to begin to talk dirty to their spouse. For all you novices, there are a number of books available that can help you develop the confidence and skills for talking dirty in the bedroom. Also, you can probably find a number of resources on the Internet with useful information. It may not seem like a really romantic gesture, but anything that spices up the action in the bedroom is really very romantic!

130. Men love lingerie- period. It's a fact and they would absolutely go wild if you were to stage a lingerie fashion show for them! You can videotape it for him so that he can enjoy you over and over again. You can take it a step further and perform a strip tease for him at the very end. Watch him loose control during your finale! Men, you can do the same for women. There are a number of different items you can don for the woman in your life. A simple bow tie and pair of Italian briefs is good enough! Whatever you do, it is between you and your spouse with the intention of increasing intimacy which will in turn nurture you love for each other.

131. No matter how the subject is approached, almost everyone has a fear of writing his or her very own love letters! The reason behind this may be that those blessed enough to be able to master the art of the written word have given the rest of us impossible shoes to fill. We believe that our love notes must be eloquent, intelligent and loaded with symbolic meaning. We struggled to find meaning in most of our high school required reading- how on earth can we possibly create our own? The good news is that *anyone* can write a successful, meaningful and touching love letter. The key to it is adding just the right amount of romance in the way that you do it!

133. When you attempt to write a love note, don't approach it with the mindset that you must write it in the way that someone like Shakespeare

would have written it (although if you have such a talent, don't let it go to waste). Love notes usually have a single intention and that is to convey how much one person loves another person. For example, if you were to walk into the bathroom and see that your spouse had left a simple message of "I Love You!" with soap or lipstick on the mirror, wouldn't you feel as if you had just received a very special love message? (It's only fair that the author of the note on the mirror should clean it up!)

133. When you feel that you simply aren't creative enough for a love note, you must remember that love notes can be communicated in a number of different ways. Walk in the door with a bunch of balloons that you wrote "I love you" on each one. Buy a package of post-it notes, write "I love you" on each one and 'decorate' the entire house with them. Write a bunch of little notes or simply "I love you" on the eggs in the refrigerator. You can also add your own personal touches by drawing funny faces or silly little sayings on the eggs.

134. If you are able to come up with a love letter you are happy with that you want to send to your spouse but you want to be able to do it in a special way, you can! Cut the letter into puzzle-shaped pieces (not too small, they shouldn't be too hard to put back together) and mail them to him or her. If you really want to make him or her work for it, only mail a single piece each day.

135. Take the time to browse the newspaper every day and look for loving, funny or even suggestive headlines and cut each one of them out. It may take several days or even weeks depending on the news, but once you have a dozen or so mail the bunch of clippings to your spouse.

136. The ultimate love note is more like a classic gesture. Find a tree that is special to both of you either in your own yard, at a favorite park, etc. and take him or her to the tree after you have carved your initials into it enclosed with a heart.

www.ingramcontent.com/pod-product-compliance
Lightning Source LLC
Chambersburg PA
CBHW070918160726
48004CB00003B/1418